39 Bamberger Theologische Studien

Bamberger Theologische Studien

Herausgegeben von Klaus Bieberstein, Jürgen Bründl,
Joachim Kügler, Thomas Laubach (Weißer) und
Konstantin Lindner

Professoren des Instituts für Katholische Theologie
der Otto-Friedrich-Universität Bamberg
im Auftrag der Bamberger Theologischen Studien e. V.

Band 39

University
of Bamberg
Press
2020

The Benefit of Inter-religious Co-operation

Examples of European and global transformation processes

Martin Affolderbach

University
of Bamberg
Press
2020

Bibliographische Information der Deutschen Nationalbibliothek
Die Deutsche Nationalbibliothek verzeichnet diese Publikation in der Deutschen Nationalbibliographie; detaillierte bibliographische Informationen sind im Internet über http://dnb.d-nb.de/ abrufbar.

Herstellung und Druck: docupoint, Magdeburg
Umschlaggestaltung: University of Bamberg Press
Umschlagbild: © Martin Affolderbach

© University of Bamberg Press, Bamberg 2020
http://www.uni-bamberg.de/ubp

ISSN: 0948-177x
ISBN: 978-3-86309-729-5 (Druckausgabe)
eISBN: 978-3-86309-730-1 (Online-Ausgabe)
URN: urn:nbn:de:bvb:473-irb-477554
DOI: http://dx.doi.org/10.20378/irb-47755

Table of Contents

Preface

Mobility has grown significantly in recent decades. Many societies, which have been shaped by culture, religion and tradition that have grown over centuries, are transforming into multi-cultural and multi-religious societies. The globalization of information and communication technologies has accelerated this development. International migration of workers, students and experts has become normal in many regions of the earth. Flight for reasons of war or persecution have brought people to other countries and has created new challenges within these societies.

Logically, religious communities are also strongly affected by these demographic and cultural developments. People of different religions who did not know each other personally in earlier decades and centuries now live door to door in many societies. This also means new challenges for the coexistence and cooperation of religious communities. On the one hand, they have become partners in a »religious market« of the respective living environment and, on the other hand, they have become global players due to their spread to numerous countries.

The articles in this volume take a closer look at a number of developments in inter-religious co-operation. What challenges and opportunities do such collaborations offer? What is the benefit of interfaith dialogues and collaborations? Are there similarities between religions that make co-operation meaningful? Do inter-religious councils and round tables own common goals or are they just the pastime of people interested in inter-cultural issues? What are the shared convictions and objectives to pursue? Where are the limits to not giving up your own identity or profile? There is no doubt that working with others has an impact on your own self-image.

The first essay »Christian–Muslim Relations in Europe. History and profile of the Journées d'Arras« describes the network of representatives of the churches in Europe on Islam which has existed for around forty years. This group addresses issues regarding the presence of Islam on this continent. In contact with Muslim partners, experiences and assessments were exchanged in order to clarify church work in a rather complex and sometimes controversial field.

»Rituals and Inter-religious Encounters. Transformations in Scandinavian countries« is the title of the second article which is devoted to current developments in a region that is historically characterized by Protestant Christianity. Three documents from Denmark, Norway and Sweden are analysed to illustrate the considerations taking place, how the presence of people of other religions and beliefs affects the form and order of church rituals.

The third article on »Inter-religious Co-operation in Europe. The example of the European Council of Religious Leaders« is intended to provide some information and assessments on efforts to build cooperation among leaders from religious communities at the European level. The development and the present character of the work of the network are of particular relevance, since it will certainly play an increasingly important role in the context of the social and political constellations in Europe in the coming years as the network is foreseen to be developed further.

The last article »Religions as Civil Actors. Current global strategies for inter-religious co-operation« analyses the current priorities and strategies of Religions for Peace International, a global network that can look back on around 50 years of existence in 2020. In August 2019, Religions for Peace International held its 10th World Assembly in Germany, in Lindau at Lake Constance, and adopted key topics and projects for the coming years. These priorities are a plea for an active and committed formation and promotion of peaceful coexistence and a responsible lifestyle within the context of the current ecological challenges.

The four articles are intended to provide an overview for interested readers and for those who are already involved in this field as well as those looking for further information, contacts and opportunities to connect. Readers familiar with the examples may miss numerous details and cross-references. Much that would have been worth mentioning had to be left out in favour of providing a succinct account. There are undoubtedly many aspects that need further examination and unanswered questions that invite further examinations and studies. Perhaps these articles encourage this.

The first three articles were published in German under the title »The religious dialogue is pushing into the church. European developments« (Der Religionsdialog drängt in die Kirche. Europäische Entwicklungen) as EZW-Texts 261, Berlin, 2019. This English publication presents a revised and updated version of the original articles.

I would like to thank everyone very cordially who has helped me with information and assessments to supplement, clarify and substantiate my personal experience in the fields described. Their names are mentioned in the respective articles. At this point I would particularly like to thank Dr. Julia Affolderbach, University of Trier, very warmly for her careful review of the English text. Dr. Ken Chitwood, Freie Universität Berlin, deserves a heartfelt thanks for useful hints. I am also very grateful to the University of Bamberg and the editors of the Bamberg Theological Studies series, mainly Prof. Dr. Konstantin Lindner and Prof. Dr. Klaus Bieberstein, for the inclusion of the volume in the series of the University of Bamberg Press.

Martin Affolderbach
Nuremberg, March 2020

Christian–Muslim Relations in Europe

History and profile of the Journées d'Arras

In some European countries Muslims can look back on a very long history of their presence, in other European countries the immigration of Muslims dates back only a few decade mainly related to labor migration in the period after the Second World War. The churches in Europe are among those actors who have very actively and intensively taken up the questions of living together with Muslims in the past decades and at the same time reconsidered their understanding of themselves in the context of other religions. The relationship between Christianity and Islam has thus become one of the most important fields of reflection on inter-religious subjects and inter-religious cooperation.

There are many areas in which a good and trusting Christian-Muslim co-operation exists. But there are also fields in which both Christian and Muslim negative stereotypes exist and the relationship is burdened by radicalization. These challenges make co-operation difficult or sometimes even impossible.

In the following, the Journées d'Arras will be used to illustrate how challenges to Christian-Muslim relations are addressed at the European level. The Journées d'Arras are a European network with a history of more than 40 years. It brings together representatives of the churches in Europe concerned with Christian-Muslim relations including experts from dialogue and study centers. The importance of this network was rated very highly by a profound connoisseur of the field, Jørgen S. Nielsen, which underlines the value of a closer examination of this network[1].

The decision taken by this group at its meeting in France in mid-2018 to reflect on the clarification of its future profile and the arrangement of co-operation[2] presents an opportunity to gather and evaluate some data and assessments[3] and then to state a few reflections on the future tasks in this field.

1. The starting point

The idea of a meeting and exchange of church representatives and experts dealing with the questions of the presence of Islam in Europe and the Christian-Muslim dialogue in the churches in Europe was first put forward in September 1977. The Roman-Catholic priest Hans Vöcking, one of the White Fathers (Catholic African missionaries), who at the time headed the Christian-Islamic Meeting and Documentation Center (CIBEDO) in Frankfurt/Main, proposed an annual meeting at European level to share and discuss questions and concerns in the various European regions.

Penelope Johnstone, a founding member of the Journées d'Arras, points out in her article[4], which describes the initial period of this network until 2004, that the »Journées Romaines", which brought together a circle of people involved in Christian-Islamic dialogue in the Mediterranean region,

---

[1] Jørgen S. Nielsen's work »Towards a European Islam« (Hampshire / London / New York 1999, p. 126) judges: »Among all the structures established out of the churches in Europe since the late 1970s the Journées d'Arras must be regarded, in all its informality, as probably the most influential of all.« He justifies this among other things with the informed contributions that the Journées d'Arras made to the expert meeting of the Conference of European Churches (CEC) on the subject of Islam 1984 in St. Pölten and to the conference of the Islam Commission of the Conference of European Churches (CEC) and the European Bishops' Conference (CCEE) 1991 in Birmingham on the subject of training theologians and church workers with regard to the dialogue with Islam.

[2] In this context, a small internal survey was carried out collecting responses from 22 participants. The results were presented to the plenary of the Journées d'Arras at its meeting 2019 in Stockholm. Some of the aspects covered in the survey will be considered later in this article.

[3] I would like to thank Joachim Finger, Switzerland, Iain MacKellar, France, and Piet Reesink, Netherlands, for some helpful hints and information.

[4] Johnstone, Penelope, The »Journées d'Arras« and the Christian-Muslim Relations, in: Islamochristiana, Pontifical Institute for Arabic and Islamic Studies (PISAI), Rome 90/2004, pp. 123–129.

has been a certain precursor. The need was seen to also establish a group with a focus especially on Europe. Father Vöcking's suggestion was presented to this circle in 1977 and once again in 1979. Both groups existed in parallel for some time, until the Journées Romaines held their last meeting in 1999.

This idea for a European meeting was taken up by the then Bishop of Arras (a town in the north of France), Mgr Gerard Huyghe, who generously invited this circle to meet in his diocese. Thus in May 1980 a group of church people charged with dialogue with Muslims from six countries met for four days in the former seminary of Arras, the later diocesan center. Because of this beginning, the meetings were called »Journées d'Arras«, a name that the network has retained until today. However, this place did not play any significant role in later years. Despite the historical beginning with impetus and support from the Catholic side, the Journées d'Arras network is ecumenical. Since 1980 the meetings have taken place annually, usually in the week after Pentecost.

From the earlier years of the Journées d'Arras it is reported[5] that the meetings discussed the situation in the respective countries and information and ideas were exchanged. The development of common goals and projects was also part of the program.

Initially, Hans Vöcking was responsible for the planning and organization of the program. In the following years, he was supported by a committee of two or three elected members. The meetings were extended by the invitation of one or two experts, who contributed with a lecture and subsequent discussion. In the following years, representatives from other countries from Scandinavia to Eastern Europe joined. Some international bodies and commissions also sent representatives to the meetings, including the World Council of Churches (WCC), based in Geneva, the Pontifical Institute for Arab and Islamic Studies (PISAI), based in Rome, and the Vatican Council for Interfaith Dialogue (PCID).

With the beginning of the retirement of Mgr Huyghe, the place of the meetings changed. In 1986 the meeting took place in Tournai, Belgium, where simultaneous translation between French and English was offered

---

[5] See also the short overview of the Journées d'Arras history, which was originally compiled by Penelope Johnstone for the homepage of the Journées d'Arras (www.muslims-and-christians.info/arras) and later supplemented, as well as the mentioned contribution by her on the beginnings of the Journées d'Arras (see footnote 4).

for the first time, then from 1988 to 1990 the meeting moved to Marseille. Since 1981, a theme was chosen for each year and contact was sought with other ecclesiastical bodies and conferences.

The basic idea and the historical beginning have given the Jornées d'Arras their specific character, which can be summarized as follows:

- The main objective of the Jornées d'Arras was and still is the exchange on issues of the Christian-Islamic dialogue and the presence of Islam in Europe.
- The participants are individuals who are concerned with these questions in the Catholic, Protestant and Orthodox churches – some are also working with universities and dialogue centers. Participants define the thematic priorities and the scope of their commitment to the Journées d'Arras themselves. There is no formal membership. Invitations are issued on the basis of a list of interested persons, which is updated from time to time.
- The initiative was taken by an individual, but was sustained by the support of a Catholic bishop. This means there is no official church mandate for this work; rather this network is a free initiative in the framework of church related ecumenical cooperation in Europe. The participation is voluntary. The Journées d'Arras are not obliged to report to the constituted churches; they do not have their own budget, but usually finance themselves by the respective participant fees for the meetings. Occasionally, there is support from the host church, a foundation or another institution.
- The fact that both English and French are conference languages of the Journées d'Arras is undoubtedly due to their origin in the French-speaking world.

2. The thematic priorities of the Journées d'Arras

The topics of the meetings since 1981 can be roughly summarized in the following groups:

(1) Theology of dialogue
- Theology of dialogue (1982, France)
- Presenting Christianity to Muslims (1991, Germany)
- Reading Bible and Qur'an (1997, Italy)
- Can we pray together? (2007, Poland)
- The image of the other (2011, Norway)
- Christian Orthodox reception of Islam (2013, Bulgaria)
- Reform and Reformation (2017, Germany)
- Interfaith spirituality (2019, Sweden)

(2) Living together
- Mixed marriages (1983, France, and 1992, Belgium)
- Muslim women (1988, France)
- Violence (2003, France)
- Polarization of attitudes (2005, Russia)
- Gender issues (2009, Germany)

(3) Muslim affairs
- The role of mosques for Muslim communities (1984, France)
- Muslim organizations in Europe (1989, France, and 1998, United Kingdom)
- Inculturation and Euro-Islam (1995, France)
- Islam on the Balkans (2000, Slovenia)
- Transnational Muslim organizations (2014, United Kingdom)
- History and culture of Muslims (2015, Austria)

(4) Education
- Muslim children in Christian schools (1981, France)
- Education of Muslim and Christian children (1986; Belgium)
- Pastoral training (1987, Belgium)
- Teaching Muslims about others (2002, Turkey)

(5) Human rights issues
- Conversion and proselytism (1985, France, and 2008, Italy)
- Human rights (1994, Austria)
- Da'wa (Muslim mission activities) (1996, France)
- Freedom of religion (1999, Germany, and 2012, Switzerland)

(6) Public life
- State, religions and secularism (1993, Belgium)
- Muslims and Christians and Nation state (2001, Sweden)
- The media and Islam (2004, The Netherlands)
- Religions and state (2006, Belgium)
- Citizenship and faith (2010, Spain)
- Situations of religions (including Judaism) (2016, The Netherlands)
- Religion and public life (2018, France)

This list shows a wide coverage of issues and a great variety of topics. A topic is usually chosen from year to year at the end of the previous meeting. The selection of a topic often takes into account the situation in the host country and the issues that the host country wishes to address.

It seems that the focus and choice of topics have not changed significantly over the years. The selection partly refers directly to the place and the background of the respective country (for example the topic »Islam on the Balkans« at the conference in Slovenia, the »Orthodox view on Islam« at the conference in Sofia, the »Religious situation in the Netherlands« at the conference in the Netherlands or the topic »Reform and Reformation« on the occasion of 500 years of Reformation at the meeting in Hanover and Lutherstadt Wittenberg). Some of the titles reflect a contemporary public debate, such as the theme »Islam and the media« at the time of the so-called cartoon crisis or the theme »Transnational Muslim organizations« with the emergence of radical Muslim groups such as »Islamic State« and others. In most cases, however, the topics are not specifically linked to current topics of public debate.

It is obvious that almost all topics are chosen from the perspective of the social majority. Therefore, the question of how to organize religious coexistence and integration is predominant. From this perspective, it seems logical that Muslim dialogue partners are always invited to contribute to a particular theme. However, they are not permanent partners in the sense that they have a say in the selection of topics. From a Muslim perspective, some urgent issues would undoubtedly be approached differently, since the problem of (religious) recognition in legal terms, the public image of religious minorities, participation in relevant aspects of society, the social situation of Muslims (areas of possible discrimination), the possibility of applying Islamic law and Sharia regulations, and other possible social conflict issues might be particularly important. The aspect of how Christian faith and a widely Christian shaped culture and society is perceived by Muslims seems to not have played a central role in the selection of topics to date.

Some titles are formulated in such a general way that in principle they go beyond the Christian-Muslim relationship (just to name a few: the relationship between state and religious communities, gender issues etc.). Only one topic, the religious situation in the Netherlands, clearly shows the inclusion of another religion, Judaism, in the program.

2.1 Country reports and the exchange of experience

In addition to these topics, country reports and the method of »Carrefour libre« are part of the established program of the annual meetings.

The method of »Carrefour libre« offers the space to present reports on projects, studies or events as well as to propose current topics to which participants can freely assign themselves according to their interest. This »format« is intended to cover an even greater variety of topics than the usually time-limited country reports allow.

Over the years, the Journées d'Arras have discussed a number of different ideas on how to present country reports in the most effective and useful way. It ranged from spontaneous contributions to written reports to be sent prior to the sessions, to reports in smaller groups of countries or to introduce abstracts in written form or as a PowerPoint presentation.

Making the country reports available to participants was also discussed suggesting the website of the Journées d'Arras could provide an opportunity to make the reports available beyond the circle of those who could participated in a meeting. In response to the intention to share the reports more widely, a grid was created for a »country data base«, according to which country profiles with various data and information were compiled and made available on the website exclusively for participants of the Journées d'Arras only. This initiative could not, however, be realized and sustained, as only a few countries generated a data base. Furthermore, updating and maintaining the website presented challenges.

2.2 The participation of Muslims in the program

Muslims are invited on a case-by-case basis to contribute to panel discussions on a specific topic as speakers or co-spokespersons or to report on Muslim life in the country or region where the meetings take place. Usually they are contact persons and partners for local or regional Christian-Muslim cooperation. The program includes almost always an excursion in the form of a visit to a mosque or a Muslim center in the vicinity of the conference venue.

3. The participants and their regional origin

The participants in the Journées d'Arras are mostly between 25 and 40 Christians of different denominations from a majority of European countries. As mentioned above, the list of interested parties administered by the secretariat of Journées d'Arras includes currently more than one hundred names. However, the circle is also relatively open, so that for example other interested persons at the respective venue are included.

3.1 Regional distribution

The evaluation of the number of participants in the meetings of the Journées d'Arras and their regional origin in the period 2007 to 2017[6] draws the following picture.

(1) Germany	52 participants
(2) Netherlands	29 participants
(3) Switzerland	27 participants
(4) Belgium	20 participants
(5) Austria	20 participants
(6) France	19 participants
(7) Great Britain	19 participants
(8) Sweden	19 participants
(9) Poland	18 participants

---

[6] The participant lists of ten meetings during this period have been evaluated.

(10) Italy	15 participants
(11) Norway	13 participants
(12) Denmark	11 participants
(13) Turkey	10 participants
(14) Finland	8 participants
(15) Russia	7 participants
(16) Bulgaria	6 participants
(17) Slovenia	3 participants
(18) Ireland	2 participants
(19) Czech Republic	1 participant

This means that 19 countries were represented at these meetings, with a wide regional spread from east to west and north to south. However, some regions of Europe are not represented or only very sporadically involved; these include the Iberian Peninsula, the Balkan countries and some parts of Eastern Europe, including the Baltic States.

The regional distribution and intensity of participation certainly allow to draw some conclusions. However, it should be borne in mind that a smaller number of participants joined relatively accidentally or spontaneously and limited in time. Nevertheless, some explanations are presented below. However, these cannot be traced back to a simple explanation scheme, but point to a quite complex and multidimensional structure.

Since the participants are Christians, on the one hand the distribution of the Christian population shares in Europe has to be considered. On the other hand, since the topic refers to Islam, the presence of Muslims in the corresponding countries might play a decisive role.

Christianity in Europe is roughly divided into Catholic majorities in the South and West, Protestant majorities in Northern Europe and Orthodox majorities more in Eastern Europe, whereby a number of Central European countries, for example Germany, have a strong mixture of Catholics and Protestants. However, some countries with significant Christian majorities are not represented in the above list of participants, such as Greece, Portugal, Romania, Spain, Ukraine and Hungary.

If the presence of Muslims in Europe is taken into consideration, the following groups of countries can be listed in terms of the proportions of Muslims[7]:

• Albania (and Turkey) have a population of over 90 per cent Muslims, and
• Bosnia-Herzegovina, Macedonia, Cyprus and Russia (in that order) count between 10 to 60 per cent.
• A proportion of Muslims between 5 and 10 per cent of the population live in Belgium, Bulgaria, Germany, France, the Netherlands, Sweden and Switzerland, followed by Denmark, Greece and the United Kingdom with percentages between 4 and 5 per cent, and Italy, Luxembourg, Norway, Serbia, Slovenia and Spain between 2 and 4 per cent.
• All other European countries have very small Muslim minorities.

A distinction must also be made between those countries in which a historical minority lives who are more or less part of the native population – this probably includes among others Albania, Bosnia, Bulgaria, Romania and Russia – and those countries in which Muslims have immigrated only in recent decades. In these states Muslims belong to the current migrant population with in some cases lower status of civil rights. This applies to Belgium, Germany, France, Great Britain, Switzerland and the Scandinavian countries.

It could be argued that more balanced representations of both religious groups within countries provides better conditions for equal living together, for example, through established structures of coexistence and dialogue. However, this is not necessarily the case, since experiences in the history of a country, current conflicts and political framework conditions also play a role. Bosnia is one European country with roughly equal Christian and Muslim populations – counting 51 percent Muslims and 31 percent Orthodox and 15 percent Catholic Christians in 2019[8] – but was not represented at any of the Journées d'Arras. The same applies to Russia with a fairly large historical Muslim minority, i.e. 14 percent Muslims beside 70

---

[7] Data taken from: Der neue Fischer Weltalmanach 2019. Zahlen, Daten, Fakten, Frankfurt am Main 2018
[8] According to: Fischer Weltalmanach 2019 (2018), p. 68.

percent Orthodox Christians and one percent each Catholic and Protestant Christians. Russia's participation was among the lowest.

Obviously, the countries with the strongest presence are those in which the immigration of Muslims has triggered public discussions and debates. The fact that such debates were and are conducted more intensively in Western democratic countries with stronger civil societies than in Eastern European countries with partly autocratic history in the last century is probably immediately obvious. A certain aspect can surely be attributed to the specific profile of Orthodox churches.

The relatively high German representation in the above list has to be seen in relation to the number of Christians in Germany. With this in mind, the participation from Belgium, the Netherlands, Austria and Switzerland is particularly remarkable. In addition, the fact that the churches in these countries, as well as in Great Britain and the Scandinavian countries, have in recent years built up a network of church Islam commissioners or those for inter-religious dialogue, which has led to a certain professionalization of this field of work which may have affected participation of these countries in the Journées d'Arras considerabley.

3.2 Confessional composition of the participants

In addition to the regional distribution of the participants, the denominational composition might also be of interest. On the basis of the evaluation of the above-mentioned lists, the following distribution can be noted:

- Catholic participants: approx. 37 %
- Protestant participants: approx. 58 %
  (incl. Anglicans and Free Churches)
- Orthodox participants: approx. 5 %

This reflects the above-mentioned commitment of the different countries and their denominational composition. The low representation of the Eastern European countries translates into a low number of Orthodox participants. Even though the Journées d'Arras had a strong Catholic representation during the initial years (cf. below in section 4 the frequency of meeting venues in France and Belgium), Protestant participants currently make up the majority.[9]

3.3 Professional background of the participants

In terms of the expertise and professional background of the participants, the following groups can be distinguished[10]; in some cases the same person can be assigned to two or more categories:

- Church counselor or mandated for the dialogue
  with Islam   approx. 12 %
- Active in a dialogue, conference or training centers   approx. 39 %
- Working in a missionary society   approx. 7 %
- Scientific researchers affiliated with universities or
  other research institutions   approx. 15 %
- Journalists or editors (e.g. for a journal)   approx. 7 %
- Practitioners or persons working at the grass-root
  level   approx. 10 %
- Others   approx. 10 %

This table shows not only the diversity of the professional backgrounds of participants, but also the different framework conditions in the participating countries. This means that the Journées d'Arras is based on a relatively broad composition of different experts.

With regard to the gender representation, the proportion of women over the past five years has been around 20 percent. It is estimated that the age of the participants is somewhat higher than in other church bodies, as in addition to full-time employees, some retired individuals are also actively involved. This subgroup, which guarantees a certain continuity and long-term transfer of experience, did not prevent the Journées d'Arras from attracting new interested individuals over the past 40 years. The

---

[9]   This ratio can also be found at the German level in terms of interreligious involvement. An evaluation of the nationwide initiative »Lade deine Nachbarn ein!« (Invite your neighbours!) has shown a similar relationship between the Christian denominations (Protestant 45%, Catholic 33%, Orthodox, Free Church, others and 22% without indication) (Bergmüller, Claudia, Final report on the evaluation of the initiative »Invite your neighbours«, Kulmbach, 2001, p. 56).

[10] Based on the knowledge and the assessment of the author.

number of participants remained surprisingly stable. The 2018 survey, mentioned at the beginning of this essay, showed that two thirds of respondents (66.6%) stated that they had attended meetings regularly for more than five years, 25 per cent even for more than 15 years.

4. The Journées d'Arras meeting venues

The locations of the Journées d'Arras are listed in historical order in the appendix (see below page 34). In terms of the frequency of meetings in different countries, the following ranking can be drawn from this list:

Country	Number of Meetings (Year)	
France	13	(1980–1985, 1988–1990, 1995, 1996, 2009, 2017)
Belgium	5	(1986, 1987, 1992, 1993, 2006)
Germany	4	(1991, 1999, 2009, 2017)
Italy	3	(1997, 2008, 2020)
United Kingdom	2	(1998, 2014)
Netherlands	2	(2004, 2016)
Austria	2	(1994, 2015)
Sweden	2	(2001, 2019)
Bulgaria	1	(2013)
Norway	1	(2011)
Poland	1	(2007)
Russia	1	(2005)
Slovakia	1	(2000)
Spain	1	(2010)[11]
Switzerland	1	(2012)
Turkey	1	(2002)

Due to the founding period of the initiative, France is the most frequent host country for the Journées d'Arras, followed by Belgium and Germany. These three countries hosted 22 of the 40 meetings (i.e., 55 percent). But the high number of meetings in France does not reflect France's current

---

[11] The conference in Madrid was organized by colleagues from Italy due to a lack of partners in Spain.

participation in the Journées d'Arras.[12] On the other hand, it is remarkable that offers have been made from a total of 16 European countries to host a meeting of the Journées d'Arras – ranging from Sweden and Norway in the north to Italy, Spain and Turkey in the south and an extension of Spain in the west and Russia in the east.

5. Structure and organisation of the Journées d'Arras

The structure and organization of the Journées d'Arras are described in a self-presentation as follows:

»A small number of people have attended regularly since 1980, while some come for one or more years. We are a network of friends and colleagues, with a sense of community and purpose, which is strengthened by our sharing in liturgy, in morning prayers, in informal conversation and in meals. The group is of a size to sit around one large table for discussion, and the atmosphere is relaxed despite the work schedule. Journées d'Arras are a small group, whose influence is probably felt more widely than we realise in the churches of Europe. We aim to inform, encourage, and assist all who are working for greater understanding between Christians and Muslims....

Although meeting only once a year, the Journées d'Arras have a small committee to keep members in touch and arrange each year's session. The Journées try to keep informed about developments in the Muslim presence and in Christian-Muslim relations throughout Europe, and to be of help to our churches. There are personal and informal links with a variety of organisations. The preparatory committee is appointed by the plenary of the annual meeting and normally composed of persons who organised the previous, the present and the meeting of the following year plus the secretary administering the list of members of Journées d'Arras and sending out the annual invitation....«

The Journées d'Arras see themselves as a collegial network in which some participants participate regularly, others only for one or more years. The sense of community is strengthened by a relaxed working atmosphere,

---

[12] Christian-Muslim cooperation currently appears to be difficult, which, according to an assessment by the Archbishops of Lyon and Dijon, has to do with the plural organization of Islam in France (cf. Vöcking, Hans, Das laizistische Frankreich und seine Muslime. Beobachtungen im Anschluss an ein Interview von Präsident Macron (Laical France and its Muslims according to an interview by President Macron), in: CIBEDO Beiträge, Frankfurt am Main, 3/2018, p. 117). A Christian-Muslim working group, which is mainly organized by the French Bishops' Conference, meets only sporadically (information by Iain McKellar, Roanne / F, June 2019).

devotions and informal exchange. The aim consists of mutual information and encouragement and the promotion of a better understanding between Christians and Muslims. Through the contacts of the participants among each other a multitude of connections to numerous church and non-church institutions have been built up.

The leadership structure consists of a planning group, which is determined by the plenum of the meetings and consists of those persons in charge of the preceding, the current and the next meeting. Additionally, a representative of the secretariat, keeping the list of those to be invited and sending out the invitations, is always present.[13] Due to the financial situation mentioned above, the management is carried out by participants or their secretariats on a part-time or honorary basis. The rolling composition of the planning group indicates that the focus is on the preparation of the annual meetings. The planning group does not have, in principle, any further mandate.

The self-description states that the Journées d'Aarras also support the work of the churches: The Journées d'Arras »are of help to the churches«. Due to the relatively loose structure of cooperation, the Journées have only twice, in 1987 and 1991, developed and adopted recommendations to the churches and a wider public.[14] The document, drawn up in 1987, is probably the result of close links with the Islam Working Group of the Conference of European Churches (CEC) and the European Bishops' Conference (CCEE). But this kind of advisory work is relatively limited to the earlier history of the Journées d'Arras and has not continued over the following decades. Thus the group's expertise served the churches largely indirectly through what the participants from the churches feed in and take back with them.

The self-description also mentions the spiritual life of the group. Morning and evening prayers as well as a concluding worship service are integral parts of each program. The fact that the venues are often, but not exclusively, church meeting centers with prayer rooms or chapels facilitates such spiritual arrangement of meetings.

---

[13] After Hans Vöcking (see above page 12f.), administration was taken over by Jan Slomp and the office of the Reformed Church in the Netherlands, followed by David Thomas, University of Birmingham. Since 2005, the secretariat has been in the church office of the Evangelical Church in Germany, Hanover, carried out by Martin Affolderbach (until 2012) and Detlef Görrig (since 2013).

[14] See also the explanation by Penelope Johnstone, op. cit. (footnote 4), pp. 126f.

6. Internal and external communication

In general, the Journée d'Arras' internal communication is more or less based on personal contact between its members, most of whom know each other through participation in the meetings and beyond. Therefore, the Journées d'Arras are more a personal network than an organizational or institutional mandated commission, although almost all members are involved in a prominent function or role in their churches or in dialogue networks. Because of this personal character, there are usually no final declarations or official statements summarizing the deliberations of a meeting. Summaries of speeches and statements depend on the mode of presentations and objectives of the keynote speakers. The same applies to the already mentioned country reports. The individual members, however, have been interested in recording and evaluating the results of the deliberations for their churches and working structures. In some cases, this has also resulted in templates for committees or contributions to journals and other publications.[15]

The Internet website of the Journées d'Arras was the medium which made accessible some basic information about the network available to a broader public, although the name »Journées d'Arras« itself does not convey any information about the content of the network and therefore presents a hurdle for interested parties to find it. For several years, a section of the website, accessible to participants via a password, held invitations to the next meetings, documents and reports. At the 2019 meeting in Sweden, it was decided to redesign this website.

In the past, there have been some efforts to use the network to provide expertise and documentation on affairs of Islam in Europe and Christian Muslim dialogue. For example, the Center for the Study of Islam & Christian-Muslim Relations in Birmingham has produced a data collection on the Christian-Muslim dialogue and some country reports from meetings of the Journées d'Arras.

---

[15] For example, in some years of the magazines »Islamochristiana«, Rome, »Religionen unterwegs« (Religions on the way), Vienna, and the magazine for Christian-Islamic Dialogue in the Netherlands »Begrip Moslims Christenen«, which was discontinued in 2016.

Occasional meetings were accompanied by press releases or talks with journalists.[16] However, the majority of the participants were more interested in an internal exchange. Public statements and declarations would have required a certain consensus among the participants as well as a strategy for communicating messages to a certain public.

7. The Journées d'Arras in the context of comparable networks

At the pan-European level, the Journées d'Arras are obviously the only ecumenical network specifically dedicated to Christian-Muslim encounters. However, in recent years the Conference of European Churches (CEC), together with the Conference of (Roman Catholic) Bishops in Europe (CCEE), set up a working group on relations with Islam in Europe.[17] This group was founded in 1987 and reappointed in 2004. It produced some documents and recommendations for the European churches.[18] In 2010 the group was not re-appointed, mainly due to restructuring on the part of the Conference of European Churches.[19]

At the European level there are other actors and networks in the field of inter-religious cooperation. However, these are not specifically related to Christian-Muslim affairs. The European Council of Religious Leaders (ECRL) was founded in 2002 as a European section within the worldwide

---

[16] One example is the 2009 conference in Bonn, Germany. The conference centre of the host, the Evangelical Church in Rhineland, established contact with the Protestant Press Service (Evangelischer Pressedienst – epd) and other journalists. Similarly, the host of the meeting in Oslo also connected with the press.

[17] Jan Slomp and Hans Vöcking presented the work of this committee in their article »The Churches and Islam in Europe« (in: Studies in Interreligious Dialogue, Leuven (21) 2011/2, pp. 211–232).

[18] Examples include the following: How can we meet Muslims? Working paper of the CEC / CCEE committee »Islam in Europe«, Geneva / St. Gallen 2003, and Christians and Muslims: Praying together? Reflections and texts. Working paper of the CEC/CCEE Committee »Islam in Europe«, Geneva / St. Gallen 2003, and Conference of European Churches and Council of European Bishops' Conferences, Committee »Islam in Europe«, Marriages between Christians and Muslims. Pastoral guidelines for Christians and churches in Europe, Geneva / St. Gallen, 1997.

[19] Jan Slomp and Hans Vöcking argued that the existence of the Journées d'Arras should have been one reason among others not to re-appoint the Commission. »Taking into consideration that several churches have well-functioning Islam desks and that the Journées d'Arras have become the ideal meeting point for sharing and comparing, the CEC and CCEE decided to discontinue its joint Islam in Europe committee.« (cf. Slomp/Vöcking 2011/12, loc. cit., (footnote 17), p. 230)

network of »Religions for Peace«[20], but it is focused on religious leaders and not limited to Christian-Muslim relations. The national structures of »Religions for Peace« also include a broader inter-religious spectrum comparable to the local, regional or national round tables (or forums) of religions.

At the level of the respective European countries there are some networks, conferences and commissions on Islamic issues or dialogue with Muslims. In Germany, for example, the Conference for Islam Affairs (Konferenz für Islamfragen) of the Protestant Churches in Germany (EKD) forms an official platform with annual meetings. Among others, this group has published a current statement on Martin Luther and Islam.[21] On the Catholic side, the Expert group on Christians and Muslims organized by the Central Committee of German Catholics (Gesprächskreis Christen und Muslime beim Zentralkomitee der deutschen Katholiken), which comprises members from both religions, should be mentioned. The Islamic-Christian Working Group (Islamisch-christliche Arbeitsgruppe), founded in 1976, was also active on the national level with representatives from both religions for about thirty years, but has discontinued its work. The Scandinavian Conference on Religious Dialogue[22], which takes place every one and a half years, is a network of Scandinavian Lutheran churches, but not limited to Islam issues.

The World Council of Churches (WCC), based in Geneva, Switzerland, has in recent years organized Christian-Muslim meetings and conferences worldwide (such as a conference series entitled »Christians and Muslims in Dialogue and Beyond«), but also various bilateral working groups and conferences with different Muslim partners.[23]

---

[20] For more details see the article in this brochure pp. 71ff.
[21] Reformation and Islam. An impulse statement of the Conference for Islam affairs of the Protestant Church in Germany (EKD), Hanover, 2016; this document is available in German as well as in English (see www.ekd.de).
[22] For more details see below pp. 55ff.
[23] Reports on respective activities can be found in the periodical of the World Council of Churches »Current Dialogue Magazine«. For example, issue 52 contains contributions to the consultation process on Christian self-understanding towards Islam.

8. Some Conclusions

Looking back on the history of the Journées d'Arras over the past forty years, its stable and consistent work over such a period is undoubtedly remarkable. On the one hand, its fairly stable membership stands out[24]. On the other hand, the number of countries involved is impressive. Furthermore, it is remarkable that this relatively loose network without full-time or part-time staff has a more stable existence than, for example, the working group officially set up by the churches in Europe. This might point to the fact that the interest in the topic is very broadly anchored and motivates cooperation and exchange, even if this obviously does not reflect a continuous institutional interest of the churches in Europe or, at least, seems not to be understood as one of their core challenges.

8.1 Islam – topic or partner?

The start of the Journeés d'Arras network with its character as mutual collegial consultation at the end of the 1970s and beginning of the 1980s, falls exactly into the time span in which, in the public debate, Muslim immigrants were not longer perceived only in respect to their ethnic and national identity but more and more with regard to their religious identity. At the same time, the churches developed an interest in the culture and religion of Islam.

The themes of the Journées d'Arras suggest that the presence of Islam was and is from the beginning not so much seen from the perspective of a religious competition, but as a challenge for the development of a society that takes another world religion seriously as a partner and wants to face up to the opportunities and problems of this coexistence. In addition, it is also specific for this network that it understands itself as an expert body among Christians on the Islam, which deals with a multitude of theological, cultural and legal aspects as well as conflict topics, rather than establishing equal participation of Muslims in the sense of a constant participation or membership.

---

[24] In the aforementioned internal survey, 46% of the respondents said they had attended the meetings for more than 10 years.

The question whether – after almost four decades of growing presence of Muslims in Europe – the time is ripe to transform the meetings preoccupied with Islam as counterpart into a form of mutual dialogue. This would, of course, mean that Muslim representatives would participate in the meetings on the same eye level and play an equally formative role. This would indeed significantly change the character of the meetings.

There are, however, some conscious and unconscious obstacles or barriers with regards to such a step. It is not clear if the participants in the Journeés d'Arras are actually interested and intend to change the network into this direction. One obstacle certainly concerns the organizational constitution and the very pluralistic internal structure of Islam, which might make it difficult, especially at the European level, to find a corresponding institutional counterpart. However, it could be argued that a rather loose network like the Journeés d'Arras is not bound to organizational structures and could freely shape a partnership with Muslim partners.

A second aspect, characteristic especially of the current development of Islam in Europe, relates to the strong internal tensions between different Muslim groups, which make a comprehensive co-operation based on trust quite difficult, if not partly impossible. In addition, it is, of course, obvious that a shared Christian and Muslim ownership of such a network would surely change the topics and the style of communication. The religious and spiritual setting of the meetings would also need a stronger coordination beyond the existing inner-Christian commonalities and an agreement about which religious elements should be taken up jointly and which require separate performances. In addition to these reasons, others may also play a role in maintaining the previous structure and objectives of the Journées d'Arras.

8.2 Mutual exchange and expertise

There is a continuing need to exchange views on the challenges posed by the presence of Islam among colleagues in a Christian framework in Europe. This obvious interest of the majority of the participants can be seen in the above-mentioned current survey of 2018, according to which participants of the Journées d'Arras particularly value both the exchange at the

European level and the expertise on the topic of Christianity and Islam (both answers received a little more than 40 percent approval each).

As far as the professional competence of the participants in the Journées d'Arras is concerned, it is made up of ecclesiastical and academic experts, some of whom can also be described as practitioners with experience in direct dialogue cooperation at the grass root level. The above-mentioned survey of participants in 2018 showed that more than 90 percent take part within the framework of their official mandate. However, many of them also cited their personal interest as a motivation to join the group. The proposal made in this survey, to consider the establishment of a legal framework for the Journées d'Arras will certainly also be discussed concerning the future design of this network.

In addition to the input provided by external experts in the form of lectures, keynote speeches, experience reports or contributions at the respective conferences, cooperation with the relevant research, documentation and dialogue centers is, of course, of great importance. In order to provide access for a broader public to those resources, contacts to individuals and institutions for different types of publications – be they journals or book publications – should also be taken into account.

It seems that such contacts are used occasionally, but not in a permanent and sustainable manner. For example, the connections that existed to Christian-Islamic Exchange and Documentation Center in Frankfurt am Main, Germany, (CIBEDO) could be reestablished and strengthened. The Journées d'Arras could also benefit from connections to the Pontifical Institute on Arabic and Islamic Studies (Pontificio Istituto di Studi Arabi and d'Islamistica (PISAI)) in Rome, relevant departments of universities, academic institutions and other partners in order to strengthen its professional expertise.

8.3 Personal exchange or consultation with the churches?

If the Journées d'Arras want to establish themselves more strongly as a consultative body for the churches, considerations would need to focus on how this goal can be achieved. Considering that many churches have set up on their level working groups or consultative commission to address different challenges, to develop recommendations or to exchange good practices, questions arise as to what work needs to be done at the European level?

There is no doubt that one of the strengths of the Journées d'Arras is to gather and share new insights and impulses from similar and different contexts through international contacts, mutual consultation and knowledge. However, this collaboration does not go beyond the current exchange of information. A more in-depth comparison and the elaboration of specific findings and challenges could only shared more widely if the Journeé d'Arras entrusted persons of its network or beyond with corresponding assignments to discuss the results and to pass them on to churches or other partners. Under the current conditions, however, this is left to academically interested persons as well as universities and study centers.

Concerning the link with church structures at the European level, it can be noted that in recent years the Journées d'Arras had invited representatives of the Conference of European Churches (CEC) and the World Council of Churches (WCC) to their meetings in order to facilitate better cooperation and links with these ecumenical bodies. To my knowledge, there was no link with the Working Group of the Community of Protestant Churches in Europe (GEKE) which produced the document on »Religious Diversity in Europe« published in 2018[25]. Further efforts are needed to establish and maintain such links and to establish closer and sustainable cooperation.

8.4 Review and looking ahead

Taking into account the development and continuous work of the Journées d'Arras over the forty years described above, it should be a worthwhile undertaking for this group to carry out a more detailed and collaborative evaluation of its work. How much insight has been gained over this period through collaboration and mutual expert advice? What issues and problems have been addressed, for what reasons and what consequences and recommendations can be derived from this, both for internal work and for societal development? At which points have Muslim dialogue partners

---

[25]   The document is available online: www.leuenberg.eu/documents.

been thematically involved, and at which themes and problems have provided the strongest points of dissent and friction?

Such an inventory would undoubtedly be of great interest in the current overall political situation in Europe. The presence of Muslims in Europe is still a continuing challenge, not only for the Christian churches, which are undergoing change in many parts of Europe, but also for numerous other sections of European societies. The developments within Islam show that this religion is presently also undergoing change and experiencing increasing inner tensions. There is no doubt that these challenges require constant attention and critical reflection. To address theses multiple challenges, the experiences and insights developed over four decades at the Journées d'Arras would be invaluable to the development of a profound vision that encourages co-operation and co-existence of Christians, Muslims and people of other faiths and convictions in the European countries drawing on.

Appendix: Locations and themes of the Journées d'Arras[26]

- 1981, Arras, France; Muslim children attending Christian schools; theological background presented by Mgr Teissier of Algeria.
- 1982, Arras, France; Questions at the level of faith which the Muslim presence puts to the Christian community. The theology of Christian-Muslim dialogue was outlined by Michael Fitzgerald, of PISAI and the then Secretariat for non-Christians.
- 1983, Arras, France; Mixed marriages, legal and pastoral aspects, and theological implications; presented by Jørgen Nielsen of Selly Oak and Guy Harpigny.
- 1984, Arras, France; Mosques, and their role for the Muslim communities in Europe; with Professor Jacques Waardenburg.
- 1985, Arras, France; Conversions, the anthropological, practical, and pastoral aspects; with G. Renier.
- 1986, Tournai, Belgium; Religious education for the younger generation, both Christian and Muslim; presented by John Shepherd, Lancaster, UK, and Andre Knockaert, Lumen Vitae, Brussels.
- 1987, Tournai, Belgium; Theological training of pastoral workers with regard to Islam; presented by Colin Chapman, Bristol, UK, and Guy Harpigny. For the first time, the Journées d'Arras decided to issue Recommendations: our churches were asked to ensure that theological and pastoral training should include instruction and awareness of Islam.
- 1988, Marseilles, France; Muslim women born or brought up in Europe; with Gé Speelman, Netherlands, and a young woman from Tunisia currently living in France.
- 1989, Marseilles, France; Muslim organisations in Europe; with Jørgen Nielsen and Jacques Waardenburg.
- 1990, Marseilles, France; Dialogue partners, following on from the previous year, but dealing more specifically with Muslim groups which relate to Christians.
- 1991, Trier, Germany; Presentation of Christianity to Muslims. After dealing for so long with Christian understanding of Islam, we wished

---

[26] This chronicle is adopted from the Journées d'Arras website (2019) and updated by the author.

to look at the situation in reverse; many Muslims genuinely want to know more about the Christian faith. The speakers were J.M. Gaudeul, Lyon, formerly of PISAI, and A. Hauser. This time too we produced Recommendations for our churches, asking for the preparation of suitable material.

- 1992, Rixensart near Brussels, Belgium; Christian-Muslim marriages and the consequences, including divorce and the upbringing of children. Presented by Andrew Wingate, of the College of the Ascension, Selly Oak, and Fr Khalil Kochassarly, a Syrian from El-Kalima, Brussels.
- 1993, Brussels, Belgium; The state, religion, and secularism (laïcité); with Jørgen Nielsen and André Coste SJ.
- 1994, Innsbruck, Austria; Christians and Muslims in Europe and human rights; with Prof Richard Potz of Vienna and Karim Demir of Heilbronn.
- 1995, Strasbourg, France; Inculturation as development towards Euro-Islam? Islamic response(s) to the challenge of western society in Europe; with Ahmed Jaballah and Jacques Waardenburg.
- 1996, Marseilles, France; Da'wa in the multireligious context of Europe; with Nico Landman and Didier Ali Bourg.
- 1997, Milan, Italy; Reading the Bible and Qur'an in pluralist societies; with Prof Aref Nayed, then a lecturer at PISAI, and Mgr Pier Fumagalli of the Ambrosiana Library.
- 1998, Birmingham, United Kingdom; Muslims organisations and the shaping of society in Europe; with Coskun Cörüz and Philip Lewis.
- 1999, Münster, Germany; The implications of religious freedom; with Halima Krausen and Stephanos Stavros.
- 2000, Celje, Slovenia; Islam in the Balkans; with Msgr Mato Zovkic, Mag. Nedzad Grabus and Tarek Mitri.
- 2001, Sigtuna, Sweden; Muslims, Christians, nation states: contributions and conflicts; with Eva Hamberg, Peter Weiderud, Pernilla Ouis and Pierre Durrani giving specialised input on Sweden.
- 2002, Istanbul, Turkey; Teaching Muslims about Others in Turkey, Teaching Muslims for Others in Europe.
- 2003, Lyon, France; Christians and Muslims faced with situations of violence, with Fouad Imarraïne of the Young Muslims of France, and P. Michel de Gigord of the diocese of Dijon.

- 2004, Hoven, The Netherlands; Islam: reporting in the Muslim and non-Muslim media, with Fouad Sidali and Theo Witvliet.
- 2005, Moscow, Russia; Polarisation of attitudes and the future of Christian-Muslim relations in Europe, with talks by Prof. A. Malashenko and Dr. A. Zhuravskiy on Islam in Russia; held at St. Andrew's Biblical Theological Institute JdA celebrated its twenty-fifth anniversary reflecting upon the past and present of Christian-Muslim relations in Europe.
- 2006, Hasselt, Belgium; theme »Relationship between Religion and the State« by reports from different countries; visit to the city of Genk and inter-religious council; lesson by Prof. Mahi Jacob, Brussels.
- 2007, Gdansk, Poland; Can Christians and Muslims pray together; talks with representatives of Muslims in Gdansk.
- 2008, Sassone/Rome, Italy; Proselytism and conversion; dialogue and evangelism; visits and talks in Rome.
- 2009, Bonn, Germany; Gender issues in Muslim-Christian relations; the topic was dealt with by a number of speakers and in working groups; visits to Muslim organizations in Cologne.
- 2010, Madrid, Spain; Citizenship and Faith in Europe; visiting the Grand Mosque in Madrid.
- 2011, Oslo, Norway; »The Image of the Other« including visits to a mosque in Oslo and with encounters with different representatives of faith traditions.
- 2012, Puidoux, Switzerland; »Religious Liberty / Liberty of Conscience« visiting the World Council of Churches, the Grand Mosque and a Muslim Center in Geneva.
- 2013, Sofia, Bulgaria; Christian Orthodox perception of Islam.
- 2014, Birmingham, United Kingdom; Transnational Muslim organizations in Europe and their impact on Christian-Muslim dialogue.
- 2015, Salzburg, Austria: History and Culture of Muslim migrants and their impact on everyday life.
- 2016, Mennorode, The Netherlands; Specific situation of religions in the Netherlands as well as of the relations among Christians, Jews and Muslims.
- 2017, Hanover/Wittenberg, Germany: Reform and Reformation within the religious traditions of Christianity and Islam.

- 2018, Pradines, France; Religion and public life (laicité).
- 2019, Marielund/Stockholm, Sweden: Christian-Muslim encounter and spiritual exchange?.
- 2020, the meeting scheduled in Rome, Italy, was postponed due to the corona crisis.

Rituals and Inter-religious Encounters
Transformations in Scandinavian countries

In Scandinavian countries, history, culture and religious identity are particularly shaped by the Lutheran Reformation. This part of Europe is currently undergoing similar changes towards religious and ideological pluralism as some other European countries, as for example Germany. This article analyzes these ongoing changes in Nordic countries and ask how the churches cope with this development. How do they understand the changes? What conclusions do they draw and what concepts do the churches develop for their future strategies?

In this essay, three documents will be analyzed to answer these questions. The documents consider how the churches can officiate baptisms, weddings and funerals in the face of the challenges the churches are confronted with due to the religious and ideological pluralism. Those official services lie not only at the core of Christian and church self-understanding, but they mark also aspects where the churches are to a high degree connected with the biography of individuals and turning points in life.

Before taking a look at these documents, the first section will outline the changes in the religious landscape of Scandinavian countries. In the second chapter, I would like to investigate the question of how the churches, but also the state and other religious communities, have responded to these changes.[1] The third part will examine the co-operation of the Scandinavian churches in respect to interfaith issues and analyze the three

---

[1] I am very grateful to Hanna Hake Barth, Oslo, Gerd Marie Ådna, Stavanger, Arngeir Langås, Hellerup/Copenhagen, and Kaj Engelhardt, Stockholm, for useful information and assessments.

current documents mentioned on the role of official services in a multi-religious environment. Finally, it summarizes how this can be assessed and
outlines lessons learnt. Which theological and practical insights can provide
new impulses? Which questions remain unanswered? Where are possibly
helpful perspectives and visions?

1. The development of religious pluralism in Scandinavian countries

In Scandinavian countries, Lutheran churches exist as majority churches
dating back to the 16th century, when Christianity in the Nordic countries
opened up to and adopted the Lutheran Reformation. In most countries
the majority situation did not originate from the Reformation movements
of the people, as in Germany and Switzerland, but mostly from policies
released by respective princes, who established Lutheranism as a generally
binding denomination. In Denmark and Sweden, the Reformation was
introduced in 1527, in Norway, then linked to Denmark, in 1536, and in
Iceland in 1539. Finland was at that time a Swedish province and therefore
followed the decisions made by Sweden. The introduction by the respective
rulers led to the development of state churches, which have survived to
the present day and fostered a strong connection between Lutheranism
and Scandinavian culture. In some parts some pre-Reformation traditions
survived. In particular, from the middle of the 19th century onward, the
codification of religious freedom initially opened up the possibility to leave
the state church in order to belong to another Christian faith community.[2]
At this time, revival movements also influenced parts of the Nordic
churches. Especially in the 19th century, considerable sections of the population emigrated to North America. Currently, the Scandinavian countries
are affected by immigration like many other parts of Europe. At the same

---

[2]   In Norway, the parliament (Storting) released the Dissenters Act (Dissenterloven) of 1845
     which allowed residents for the first time that to become a member of a Christian com-
     munity outside the Lutheran Church. This law was only replaced in 1964 by a law on gen-
     eral religious freedom (Ingun Montgomery, Norway, in: Theologische Realencyclopädie
     (TRE), Vol. 24, Berlin / New York 1994, p 651). Regarding the corresponding legal devel-
     opment in Sweden, see the explanations by Jarlett, Anders, in: Sweden III, in: TRE, Vol.
     30, 1999, pp 662ff.

time, the relationship between state and churches is also in a process of change.

1.1 Demographic development and religious affiliation

Sweden is by far the largest Scandinavian country in terms of population, whose number of inhabitants increased from 9.18 million to 10.12 million between 2008 and 2018 as a result of birth rate and immigration.[3] Religious affiliation has changed significantly over the past 30 years. In the year 1990, 95 percent of the 8.5 million residents belonged to the Lutheran state church (which amounts to 8.07 million persons) and 188,600 were Catholic and 16,000 Jewish fellow citizens (corresponding to about 2 per cent). In 2019, only 66 percent were still members of the Church of Sweden, alongside 6 percent Muslims; Catholic Christians and other religious minorities make up 2 percent.[4] For the year 2020, 6.2 million Christians are forecast for Sweden, which would correspond to a share of approximately 60 percent of the population. At the same time however, 2.9 million persons don't have any formal religious affiliation, which corresponds to approximately 28 percent of the population. In addition, 640,000 Muslims and a good 100,000 people of other religious groups are predicted for the mentioned year.[5] The membership statistics of the Church of Sweden confirm this picture by indicating 7.63 million members in 1990 and 5.99 million in 2017.[6]

In Norway, a similar development can be observed. The population grew from 4.73 million in 2008 to 5.29 million in 2018[7], largely as a result of immigration since the late 1990s, but especially between 2005 and 2016, with a peak in refugee immigration in 2015.[8] With regard to religious affil-

---

[3]　See the Eurostat database (www.ec.europa.eu/eurostat); the Statista database (www.de.statista.com) shows slightly higher figures, 9.26 million for 2008 and 10.23 million for 2018. (accessed in May 2019).

[4]　See Fischer Weltalmanach 1990, Frankfurt a. M. 1989, and Der neue Fischer Weltalmanach 2019, Frankfurt a. M., 2018; Eurostat (see footnote 3) does not provide figures on religious affiliation.

[5]　See Statista (footnote 3).

[6]　Svenska kyrkans medlemsutveckling år 1972–2017, see: www.svenskakyrkan.se/filer/ Medlemmar i Svenska kyrkan 1972–2017, p 2.

[7]　According to Eurostat (see footnote 3); Statista (see footnote 3) also reports slightly higher figures here indicating 4.79 million for 2008 and 5.32 million for 2018.

[8]　According to www.ssb.no/en/befolkning the proportion of migrants there is given as

iation, the Lutheran state church accounted for 87.8 percent and minorities
of 18,000 Catholics and 1,000 persons of Jewish faith in 1990. This has
changed to 73 percent Lutherans, 3 percent Muslims and 2 percent
Catholics for the year 2019.[9]

Population growth in Denmark between 2008 and 2018 amounts to
5.5 percent, from 5.48 million in 2008 to 5.78 million in 2018.[10] This
growth is only about half of the one in Sweden (10.5 percent) and Norway
(11.1 percent). During this period, the proportion of foreigners rose from
5.45 percent in 2008 to 8.75 percent.[11] In terms of religious affiliation,
members of the Lutheran Church declined from 81 percent of the population in 2012 to 77 percent in 2019. During the same period, the number
of Muslims rose from 4 to 5 percent.[12] It can be assumed that, like in the
countries described above, an increasing proportion of the population in
Denmark does not belong to any religion.

In Finland, which has seen a population increase from 5.30 million in
2008 to 5.51 million in 2018[13], 91.5 percent of the population were members
of the Lutheran state church in 1990. Around 59,000 people belonged to
the Orthodox Church (also a state church), around 3,300 to the Catholic
Church, around 1,300 to the Jewish faith and around 800 to Islam.[14] In
2008 the figures dropped to 81 percent Lutherans, although it should be
noted that 17 percent of the population is now reported as without any religious affiliation. These figures continue to change with 73 percent of the
population being Lutheran, 24 percent without religion and others ac-
counting for 1 percent or less, in 2019.

Iceland's development in the period 2008 to 2018 also includes an increasing proportion of foreigners, from 7.4 percent to 10.8 percent, with a
total population of 357,000 (at the end of 2018).[15] However, due to the national origin of migrants, the proportion of Muslims is very low. In 2012,
the proportion of the Lutheran population was 79 percent, which declined

---

16.3% of the population (cut-off date of 1 January 2016), whereby only Muslim member-
ships are counted, which maybe include only half of the Muslims residents.

[9]   Cf. Fischer Weltatlas 2019 (see footnote 4).
[10]   According to Eurostat (see footnote 3); Statista (see footnote 3) indicates the same figures.
[11]   Cf. Statista (see footnote 3).
[12]   Cf. Fischer Weltatlas 2019 (see footnote 4).
[13]   According to Eurostat (see footnote 3).
[14]   According to Fischer Weltatlas 1990, 2012 (indicating the figures from 2008) and 2019
[15]   Eurostat (see footnote 3) indicates a population growth from 2008 to 2018 of 0.31 million
       to 0.35 million.

to 77 percent by 2019. The proportion of the Catholic population rose from 3 to 4 percent due to immigration and the number of people with non-religious affiliation increased from 3 to 6 percent. Other denominations and religions form very small minorities.[16]

As far as population development and religious classification in Scandinavia are concerned, Lutheran majority churches but also appreciable minorities of other denominations and religions have established themselves in most countries allowing religiously plural societies to develop alongside the continuing majority of Lutherans. The share of foreigners, which currently amount for an averages of 7.79 percent in the European Union, accounts for 8.75 percent in Sweden and Denmark. This makes up the 12th and 13th position in the EU ranking, compared with only 4.5 percent in Finland and 11.69 percent in Germany.[17]

In addition to the establishment of other denominations and religions, the growing number of people who are not religiously affiliated is also remarkable. However, these do not only originate from the domestic population, but are also to be found among migrants. It is estimated, for example, that about half of the Muslims in Sweden are secular Muslims.[18]

These developments cannot be interpreted and analyzed in more detail in this essay. However, a number of factors may have led to these changes. Secularization in the sense of an emancipation of various areas of life from religious ties is likely to be one factor with a longer historical impact. Individualization, globalization, mobility and urbanization are other factors that have become increasingly important in recent decades. A further aspect, as explained above, is the changed composition of the population, which increasingly leads to »hybrid identities« due to the immigration of people from other countries and cultures. Internal migration within Europe, but also the immigration of labor migrants, are factors that have played a role since the 1950s.

The influx of refugees and asylum seekers has triggered public controversy in many countries. A peak was reached in 2015 with the influx of asylum seekers, mainly from Syria, Iraq and Turkey, which led to a further restriction of asylum rights in many countries. Denmark introduced con-

---

[16] According to Fischer Weltalmanach 2012 and 2019.
[17] Cf. Statista (see footnote 3).
[18] Cf. Berglund, Jenny, Teaching Islam. Islamic Religious Education in Sweden, Münster / New York / München / Berlin 2010, p. 23.

trols at the border to Germany and reinforced the fortifications along this frontier. Sweden, which in 2017 showed the highest rate in Europe – counting 24 recognized asylum seekers per 1,000 inhabitants –[19] also tightened its asylum law and cut payments to rejected asylum seekers.

Right-wing populist parties and groups had already emerged in the Scandinavian countries in the 1990s. Within these groups the emphasis on conservative values and nationalist orientation was accompanied by varying degrees of xenophobia and the rejection of globalization and European cooperation. Founded in 1973, the Progressive Party (Fremskrittspartiet) has been one of the governing parties since 2013, even though it lost votes nationwide in the national parliament (Storting) election of 2017. The Danish People's Party (founded in 1995) was the second strongest party in the Danish Volketing from 2015 to 2019. In Sweden, the Swedish Democrats (Sverigedemokraterna), founded in 1988, have been represented in the national parliament (Riksdag) since 2018 (with 62 MPs). The True Finns (Perussuomalaiset; since 2012: The Finns), founded in 1995, achieved government participation until their split in 2017.

This development in the political convictions of the population shows that the issues of immigration, asylum and, above all, the ethnic and cultural pluralization of societies are among the most controversial and emotionally charged topics of public debate. This often makes it more difficult to deal with the challenges involved in an objective manner.

1.2 Role and status of religious communities

Besides the demographic changes, the development of the religious landscape also correlates with status of religious organisations and the public role of religious communities in the respective countries. In Scandinavian countries, the state church tradition results in a special setting, which needs to be taken into account, as it differs between countries.

Denmark has a Lutheran people's church, in which the historical model of a state church is still most clearly preserved. The status of the Lutheran Church as a »Danish People's Church« (Folkekirken) is regulated in paragraph 4 of the Danish Constitution and assures the Church of the support

---

[19] Cf. Der neue Fischer Weltalmanach 2019, p. 403.

of the state.[20] At the same time the church also performs some state administrative tasks (role of the registry office and keeping registers of residents). However, the Constitution provides for full religious freedom[21] and a ban on discrimination based on religion. Other religious communities can obtain the status of »recognized religious communities«, but receive no financial support from the state. The historic role of the Royal House as the spiritual head of the Church has been exercised since 1849 by the Church Ministry in cooperation with the parliament (Folketing) and the government. The bishops of the ten Danish dioceses supervise the legally autonomous Lutheran congregations, including the aforementioned communal functions. However, the bishops have no power to make public statements, so that the Danish People's Church has no mandate in this respect. State religious education is a compulsory subject from which pupils who are not church members can only be partially exempt.

In Sweden and Norway the close relationship between state and church has undergone lasting changes in recent years.[22] In Sweden, the separation of state and church came into force in the year 2000 based on a 1995 law, after legal changes had already been made in the previous decades – for example by the Freedom of Religion Act of 1951 – and commissions had come forward with proposals for restructuring. With the change at the turn of the millennium, the Swedish Church (Svenka Kyrkan) lost its role as a state authority and received the legal status of a »registered religious community«, which can also be granted to other religious communities.[23] With this change, Sweden follows the German model assigning public corporation status to the churches. Clerics are no longer civil servants, and contributions to the Church are no longer collected in the form of church taxes. The cemetery system, however, remains under the administration of the Church of Sweden.

Norway followed the Swedish example in 2012. After numerous preliminary plans, a synod of the Lutheran Church (Kirkemøtet) had already

---

[20]   Cf. Hoburg, Ralf, Protestantismus und Europa. Erwägungen für eine Kirche der Konfessionen. Geschichte, Modelle, Aufgaben (Protestantism and Europe. Considerations for a Church of Denominations. History, models, tasks), Berlin 1999, pp. 134ff.

[21]   This was guaranteed with the introduction of a democratic constitution through the Basic Law of 1849. For church history in Denmark, see also Schwarz Lausten, Martin, Denmark I, in: TRE, Vol. 8, 1981, pp. 300–317.

[22]   Cf. Hoburg, Ralf (see footnote 20), pp. 136ff.

[23]   Cf. Jarlett, Anders, Schweden III (see footnote 2), p. 674.

been established in 1985, which received for example the right to appoint clergy. New legislation on the relationship between the state and the churches or religious communities is currently being drafted[24] to regulate whether all religious communities will be subject to the same legal provisions or whether the Lutheran Church will retain special rights in some areas. The size of a congregation in terms of membership determines the amount of state support allocated.[25] The right of free exercise of religion exists since 1851. Similar to Sweden, revival movements within the churches play a significant role and shape church life in some parts of the country. It should also be mentioned that in Norway organized humanism plays a role alongside religious communities. The humanist association »Human-Etisk Forbund«, founded in 1956, has about 86,000 members (approx. 1.7 percent of the population) and reaches a noticeable size. The humanistic confirmation ritual is popular in cities, but less so in rural areas.[26]

The Republic of Finland sees itself as a religiously neutral state, in whose constitution freedom of religion was enshrined in 1923. There are two state churches, the Evangelical Lutheran Church and the Finnish Orthodox Church, which receive financial contributions from the state. The number of non-Christian religious minorities is very small, at about 2 percent of the population, so that the various Christian denominations and groups play a much greater role in terms of numbers.[27] Many of the Muslims living in the country are Tatars who immigrated in the 19th century. As a result, Muslims do not play the same role in Finland as in the other Scandinavian countries.

Iceland has also had an Evangelical Lutheran Church (Íslenska þjóðkirkjan) since the Reformation period. According to Article 62 of the Constitution of the Republic of Iceland of 1944, the Evangelical Lutheran Church

---

[24]   The government received only partial recommendations from the report on the future role of communities of faith and belief, which was prepared by Sturla Stålsett and submitted in 2013.

[25]   A minimum membership of 50 people to secure state funding was set in June 2019. In regard to cemeteries, municipal and church authorities are foreseen to work together to ensure adequate graves for members of different faiths.

[26]   According to www.fritanke.no, 19 percent of all 14-year-olds are said to have participated in a humanistic »confirmation« in Norway in 2018.

[27]   Cf. Ketola, Kimmo / Martikainen, Tuomas, The Religions in Finland Project, in: Mortensen, Viggo (Hg.), Religion & Society. Crossdisciplinary European Perspectives, Aarhus 2006, pp. 81–89; see also www.uskonnot.fi/english.

is understood as a state-supported people's church. Freedom of religion has been guaranteed since 1874. Membership of the People's Church fell from 96 percent in 1994 to 67 percent in 2018. This decline is considered to be also attributed to internal church problems. The small Catholic Church in Iceland is not only registering resignations but also an immigration of Catholics from the Philippines, Poland and the Baltic States.[28] According to a survey carried out in 2012, 31 percent of Icelanders are considered non-religious, which is a remarkably high figure worldwide. In addition to some free churches with significant membership, Muslims and Buddhists are very small religious minorities amounting to 0.3 percent of the population each.

The historically strong link between (Lutheran) Christianity and national identity in the Nordic churches still shapes the consciousness and sensibility of many people in these countries. In earlier centuries, this had its expression in the self-evident membership in the Lutheran Church, which partly consisted in a commitment to baptism (and confirmation). This seems to be still visible when it is reported that migrants are sought for baptism because they want to »become Swedish«.[29] The Swedish church's keeping of the personal registration registers (folkbokföring) until 1991 illustrates a further aspect of such an interlocking of civil society and church. Against this background the change to a multi-religious society may represent a clearer transformation of self-understanding than in some other countries.

Despite some differences in the Nordic churches, all countries experience a decline in membership of the Lutheran popular churches in favour of those who are not religiously bound. The immigration of Muslims plays a role in Denmark, Norway and Sweden, but less so in Finland and Iceland. These two countries are therefore not the focus of the following discussion, but will marginally be considered.

---

[28] Cf. Gessler, Philipp, Auf kargem Boden. Das Christentum in Island nimmt ab – aber Hoffnung ist angebracht (On barren ground. Christianity in Iceland is declining – but hope is appropriate), in: Zeitzeichen. Evangelische Kommentare zu Religion und Gesellschaft, 1/2019, pp. 53–58.

[29] Cf. De kyrkliga handlingarna i en mångreligiös kontext. Ett brev från Svenska kyrkans biskopar, Uppsala, 2012, p. 32.

2. Structural and conceptual responses to development

The churches have responded to the described developments gradually in structural and conceptual terms. Project and dialogue groups have emerged in numerous church congregations, especially in urban areas. These groups concern both social assistance for immigrants and dialogue and exchange on cultural and religious issues. Numerous working groups, committees and conferences seek to address the challenges of an ethnically and religiously pluralistic society and jobs have been created and clergymen and people with other qualifications have been employed full-time or part-time, often supported by numerous volunteers who are involved in this new field of work.

2.1 Structural responses

Over the past centuries Denmark represented a religiously and ethnically very homogeneous society but within the church there were considerable tensions between different groupings, for example between Grundtvigianism, the representatives of dialectical theology (Tidehverv), the Inner Mission and Pietist and revivalist movements.[30] The changes of the last decades resulted in an increased share of Muslims and an influence of Eastern religions. It is assumed that »at least 20% of the population today believe in reincarnation and that today there are far more alternative healers in Denmark than practicing doctors«[31].

Similar to Germany, the beginnings of inter religious work can be traced back to the efforts of free Christian organizations. The mission societies, including the Østerlandmission, Danish Church Mission in Arabia, Sudanmission and others, provided experiences of contact with other religions on different continents, which were taken up in part by the Danish Mission Society (DMS) in the sense that it established a first meeting center for migrants in Vesterbro, a district of Copenhagen, in the 1980s.

---

[30] This development is summarized by Mogensen, Mogens S., in: Mogensen, Mogens S., Church and Interreligious Dialogue in Denmark, (Manuscript) Breklum 2011 (Source: www.academia.edu).
[31] Mogensen, Mogens S., op. cit., p. 1; »Healer« means religious healers and people who offer alternative medical treatment.

Numerous church congregations subsequently became involved in this field of work, for example, with inter-religious meals and other activities. In 1996 a group of Christians and Muslims founded an Islamic-Christian Study Centre (Center for Sameksistens – Islamisk-Kristent Studiecenter) in Copenhagen[32]. Several Lutheran dioceses followed with the establishment of regional commissions on Islamic affairs. In 2002, eight of the ten dioceses of the Lutheran church in Denmark established the Institute for the People's Church and Religious Dialogue (Stiftssamarbejdet Folkekirke og Religionsmøde). As some Muslims converted to Christianity, material for lessons to prepare them for baptism was needed (published in 2010 under the title »The Way of Christ«).

The violent reactions in some Muslim countries triggered by the publication of the Islamic cartoons in Jyllands-Posten in 2006 and the subsequent public debate led to further efforts, which, according to Mogens S. Mogensen, led to the reaction on the Muslim side to ask: »Why only now?«, and the establishment of a Muslim-Christian discussion forum lead by representatives from both sides. It also triggered the foundation of a network of members of the People's Church in Denmark who are very critical towards Islam.[33]

Besides the contacts to Islam, the study of new-religious movements as well as Eastern religions plays a considerable role in Denmark. This led to strengthened offers in the area of Christian spirituality, but also to further training offers (for example by the Theological-Pedagogical Center Lögumkloster and the mission society Areopagos[34]), in order to qualify clergy and other church people interested and involved in this field of work.

In Norway, the Lutheran Church took the initiative to first Christian-Muslim contact talks which took place in Oslo in 1988. The main topics of these talks were the changes towards a multicultural society in Norway, but also the issues of recognition and mutual respect. Out of these beginnings, the formally established cooperation of a contact group between the Islamic Council of Norway and the Council for Ecumenical and Inter-

---

[32] The initiator and director of the center is the pastor Dr. Lissi Rasmussen; current information can be found on www.ikstudiecenter.dk.

[33] In Norway there were less violent reactions from the Muslim side, as contacts already existed which were used for discussions immediately after the cartoons had been published.

[34] See further informationen on www.loegumkloster-refugium.dk and www.dansk.areopagos.dk/dialog/.

national Relations of the Lutheran Church (Kontaktgruppa for Islamsk Råd Norge og Mellomkirkelig Råd for Den Norske Kirke) emerged in 1993. This contact group drew up three joint declarations (Felleserklæringene).

Following a period of restructuring on the Muslim side, the cooperation in recent years has been put on a new footing. The aforementioned Areopagos Foundation, which has been working as a Nordic Christian mission among Buddhists since 1922 and which sees itself today as a dialogue forum, founded the Emmaus Dialogue Centre (Emmaus. Senter for dialog og spiritualitet) in Oslo in 1991[35]. This center was converted into a Church Dialogue Centre (Kirkelig dialogsenter) of the diocese of Oslo of the Lutheran Church in 2010 and carries out national responsibilities on behalf of the Interchurch Council (Mellomkirkelig råd for Den norske kirke). Additional church dialogue centers have been established since 2011 in Bergen, Stavanger, Trondheim and Drammen. One more is planned for Tromsø. The dioceses are recommended to appoint dialogue commissioners. This work strengthens numerous inter-religious contacts, projects and co-operations that have developed in recent years, especially in urban areas. For example, the cooperation between the municipality and the parish in Nærbø on the southwest coast of Norway carried out a remarkable project.

In Norway ideological groups, especially humanists, play a more important social role than in other countries. The first official talks between the Church and the Humanists were established in 1985, prompted by the issue of the content of religious education in schools. The Council for Co-operation between Faith and Worldview Communities (Samarbeidsrådet for tros- og livssynssamfunn[36]) was founded in 1996 and is supported by government grants. The Council also works on ethical and human rights issues and intends to promote understanding and tolerance between religious and ideological groups. In addition to the churches and the Humanist Association of Norway, Sunni and Shiite Muslims are also represented in this Council.

In Sweden, Bishop Tor Andræ and Bishop Natan Söderblom developed inter-religious approaches in the first decades of the 20th century. Bishop Andræ got in contact to mystical traditions of Islam and Bishop Söderblom,

---

[35] See www.kirkeligdialogsenter.no.
[36] The members of the council can be found on www.trooglivssyn.no/om-oss/#medlemmer.

who is known for his ecumenical involvement, to Judaism[37]. However, more sustainable contacts to Judaism did not emerge until the 1970s and to Islam not until the 1980s.

In 1995 the Church Assembly of the Swedish Church decided on a multi-year project on encounter with Islam. As a result, numerous groups and projects were formed at the local level, which established contacts with refugees and people of other languages, religions and origins at universities, in hospitals, prisons, in accommodation centers for asylum seekers and migrants or through the establishment of language cafés, women's groups or in the area of children and youth activities. Such groups and projects reach from Malmö in southern Sweden to Haparanda at the border to Finland. Many activities have led to permanent contacts between church communities and mosques. In the Stockholm district of Fisksätra, the Christian-Islamic meeting center »Guds hus« (House of God) emerged from a cooperation established in the year 2000. In addition, the immigration of bigger numbers of refugees in 2015 led to numerous spontaneous projects and an intensification of contacts.

All 13 dioceses of the Church of Sweden have nowadays employed people who are charged with inter-religious affairs. The Center for Inter-religious Dialogue in Stockholm, founded in 2008, has taken over the task of organizing regular exchanges between these experts. In 1998, a fire broke out in a discotheque in Gothenburg where 63 young people from numerous countries lost their lives. This was a trigger to intensify inter-religious contacts and work. Gothenburg has an inter-religious center since 2012. In the diocese of Linköping, an international book publication on good practices and experiences of inter-religious activities was produced in cooperation with partners in England.[38] At the national level, the Swedish Inter-religious Council (Sveriges interreligiösa råd), a body of representatives of churches, Islam, Judaism, Buddhism, Baha'i, Sikh, Hinduism, Mandeans and Alevis who meet four times a year, was formed in 2010 on

---

[37] In regard to developments in Sweden cf. Lööv Roos, Peter, Svenska kyrkans interreligiösa sammanhang, Uppsala 2016; this overview of inter-religious activities in the Swedish Church, created by Peter Lööv Roos, goes back to a decision of the Church Assembly in 2014 and was developed on the basis of intensive research in 2015 and 2016.

[38] Myrelid, Parnilla / Wingate, Andrew (ed.), Why Interfaith? Stories, Reflections and Chalanges From Recent Engagements in Northern Europe, London 2016; this booklet was also published in Swedish under the title: Våga Möta. Kyrkans kallelse i ett mångreligiöst Europa, Skellefteå, 2016.

the initiative of the Lutheran Archbishop. Comparable regional networks and inter-religious councils have been established in Gothenburg, Örebro, Norrköping and other places. In many regions there are opportunities for exchange and further training for church staff and others who are active in the inter-religious field.

In Finland, a forum for religious encounters has been established in January 2011 under the name »Uskontojen yhteistyö Suomessa ry – USKOT-foorumi / Religionernas samarbete i Finland rf – RESA-forumet«, consisting of Christian, Jewish and Islamic representatives.[39] Despite the small numbers of members of other faith communities alongside the Lutheran majority church. The aim of the cooperation is to promote social peace, freedom of religion and inter-religious dialogue.

Obviously, in some Scandinavian countries, the development towards a culturally and religiously pluralistic society and a change in the relationship between state and church is accompanied by a change in attitude and policies on the part of the state and the municipalities. Norway reports that the separation of state and church has not led to the self-understanding of a religiously neutral state, but to an understanding of society that is open to religious communities (»Det livssynsåpne samfunn«[40]). In Denmark, »social diversity« concepts of a multi-religious or multicultural society are avoided and instead the term »social cohesion« (samhørighed) is used. Also the role of the churches in the clarification and mediation of conflicts is more strongly perceived and appreciated by the state.

2.2 Conceptual answers

In the Nordic churches, approaching inter-religious issues from a conceptual perspective started already several decades ago with the churches having also sought contact and exchange at the international level.[41]

---

[39] See www.ekumenia.fi.
[40] This wording is also the title of the national report commissioned by the Norwegian Ministry of Culture and developed under the direction of Sturla Stålsett and submitted in 2013 (www.regjeringen.no/no/dokumentarkiv); cf. footnote 24.
[41] Documents of the Lutheran churches in Sweden and Norway are described in the document of the Community of Protestant Churches in Europe (CPCE), Protestant Perspectives on Religious Plurality in Europe, Basel 2018, pp. 18f; concerning the Swedish debate linked to international partners cf. also Lööv Roos, Peter, op. Cit. (footnote 37), p. 27ff.

With regard to ecumenical cooperation among churches in Northern Europe on inter-religious issues the elaboration of the document »Guidelines for Encounters with Other Religions for Churches of the Porvoo Church Fellowship« signifies a striking milestone. The so called Porvoo Communion[42] is a church fellowship which includes Anglican and Lutheran churches, especially in Great Britain, Scandinavia and the Baltic States. At the end of 2003 the document was published, which takes social change by recent immigration and ethnic and cultural diversity as well as current migration movements as starting point to address associated challenges. The religious, spiritual and ideological diversity is a common theological task of the participating churches. Twelve points were recorded in the document: a long-term need to build trust, to speak about others truthfully and in a self-critical manner, to witness one's own faith, to come together before God, to seek contact to multi-religious communities, to use opportunities for learning and teaching, to support inter-religious families and partnerships, to work together for the common good, to include women and men, to pay due attention to the international context, to stand up for religious freedom and to deal responsibly with conversion.

In 2001, the Christian churches in Europe adopted the »Charta Oecumenica. Guidelines for Growing Cooperation among Churches in Europe«[43], which describes the relationship to Islam in paragraph 11 as follows: »*We commit ourselves to treat Muslims with esteem and to work together with Muslims on common concerns.*« With reference to this passage, the Church Chancellery of the Swedish Church, at the request of the 2004 Church Assembly, published a handbook entitled »The most important things about Islam. Fifteen things Christians should know about Islam«[44], which explains basic Islamic and Arabic terms – especially those that may be subject to misunderstanding.

---

[42] This Church Communion was established in the city of Porvoo (in Swedish Borgå) in 1992 which is situated in south Finland east of Helsinki and owns a seat of a Lutheran Bishop. The mentioned document can be found on the Porvoo Community website (www.porvoocommunion.org): Porvoo Communion Consultation on Inter Faith Relations, Oslo, 30th November – 3rd December 2003, Guidelines for Inter Faith Encounter in the Churches of the Porvoo Communion. A Swedish version can be found in the brochure »Religionsmöte. Ekumeniska document«, Katrin Åmell (ed), Stockholm, 2006, pp. 50–57.

[43] Gevena / St. Gallen, 2001.

[44] Viktigt att veta om islam. Femton saker som kristna bör veta om islam, Svenska kyrkan, Kyrkokansliet, 2004, in: Religionsmöte, loc cit. (footnote 42), pp. 58–64; the authors are Kajsa Ahlstrand and Cajsa Sandgren Bengtsson.

From 2003 to 2005 a working group of the Swedish Christian Council (Sveriges Kristna Råd) in cooperation with the Sigtuna Foundation (Sigtunastiftelsen), a dialogue and conference center between Stockholm and Uppsala, chaired by the Catholic nun Katrin Åmell, addressed religion-theological issues and published the two mentioned documents as a manual for the participating churches[45]. This brochure included also further documents of the World Council of Churches[46] and the Islam Commission of the Conference of European Churches and the European (Catholic) Bishops' Conference[47]. It was intended to show more clearly that religions, in view of fundamental similarities, for example with regard to the so-called Golden Rule, and should cooperate more closely and overcome mutual misunderstandings and prejudices.

In 2006, the General Synod of the Lutheran Church of Norway dealt with the relationship with other religions and decided on a manual for inter-religious encounters (»Veiledning i religionsmøte«).[48] The Council for Ecumenical and International Relations of the Church of Norway followed in 2008 with a paper on guidelines for inter-religious relations. In 2016, the Council of the Church of Norway addressed the issue of interfaith dialogue and adopted a unanimous motion which provides the basis for the consolidation of dialogue work, especially with regard to the above-mentioned expansion of church dialogue centers and dialogue commissioners.

---

[45] Religionsmöte, loc. cit. (see footnote 42).
[46] A brief overview over the development of this topic in the World Council of Churches can be found in Oxley, Simon, Ökumenischer Rat der Kirchen und interreligiöses Lernen (World Council of Churches and Interreligious Learning), in: Schreiner, Peter / Sieg, Ursula / Elsenbast, Volker (ed.), Handbuch interreligiösen Lernen (Handbook on Interreligious Learning), Gütersloh 2005, pp. 714–718.
[47] This committee, founded in 1987, also held a Europe-wide Christian-Islamic conference in 2001 on the topic »Christians and Muslims in Europe. Responsibility and Religious Obligation in a Pluralistic Society« (documented in: Cristiani e Musulmani in Europe, Religioni e sete nel mondo, Issue 21, Bologna, 2001/2002; partly texts in four languages).
[48] An English version of the text can be found (as pdf-file) on www.kirken.no/globalassets

3. Nordic cooperation on interfaith issues

An exchange on inter-religious issues had already existed between Denmark and Norway for a considerable time.[49] The cooperation and exchange within the Scandinavian Lutheran churches intensified from 2009 onward with those charged with inter-religious issues or active in the inter-religious field meeting alternately in one of the participating countries for conferences every one and a half years. This initiative was launched by the Center for Religious Dialogue in Stockholm[50] which together with other Lutheran churches in Scandinavia, saw a need to discuss and clarify theological issues arising in inter-religious dialogue in cooperation with church practitioners and academics.[51]

The first of these meetings took place in Stockholm in December 2009 under the programmatic title: »The Nordic folk churches in a multi-religious society« (De nordiske folkekirker i et flerreligiøst samfund). The invitation outlined the practical and theological challenge for the Nordic people's churches that the population no longer belonged to the church uniformly and that there were no longer only Christians. What this meant for Christian identity required intensified exchange. Reports have been submitted by the Center for Religious Dialogue, Stockholm, the Danish Center for People's Church and Religious Encounter (Stiftssamarbejdet Folkekirke og Religionsmøde), Frederiksberg/Copenhagen, and the Emmaus Centre in Oslo.

»The Nordic churches in dialogue« was the theme of the following meeting in Oslo in February 2011, which involved conversations with the Norwegian Council for Religions and Worldview Communities. Newly published material from Denmark for baptismal instruction for migrants was presented. In addition to country reports from Denmark, Norway and Sweden, there were also reports from Finland and Iceland.

In August 2012, the meeting in Copenhagen on »Challenges and Opportunities in a Multicultural Society« (Udfordringer og muligheder i det multikulturelle samfund) focused on questions of what a multi-religious

---

[49] Oddbjørn Leirvik, Faculty of Theology at the University of Oslo, was one of the main organizers.
[50] Centrum för religionsdialog Stockhom stift; see www.svenskakyrkan.se/stockholmsstift
[51] Cf. Egnell, Helene, Från fastspickade teser till öppna dörrar, in: Svenska Kyrkotidning 6/2015, pp. 193–195.

society could be built on and how to organize coexistence and dialogue. At this and at following meetings, the country reports also included a report from Germany.

The meeting in March 2014 in Sigtuna, Sweden, returned to the focus of the first conference with an explicit Lutheran approach in view of the Reformation anniversary in 2017: »The Nordic People's Churches in a Multi-religious Society – a Lutheran Perspective« (Nordiska folkkyrkor i ett mångreligiöst samhälle – lutherska perspective). The meeting included a visit to a Christian-Muslim project and a keynote on the Christian-Jewish dialogue, as it explored whether the fundamental Reformation idea of justification by grace can also be found in other religions[52].

Finland hosted the conference in Helsinki in September 2015. In contrast to the other meetings where the speakers used their Danish, Norwegian or Swedish mother tongue, this meeting was held in English to help Finnish participants to join in. The title »The Nordic Lutheran Folk Churches and New Spirituality« broadened the view of the religious dialogue to a variety of religious groups and movements, including esoteric groups and different forms of new spirituality within the churches.

The conference in Stavanger, Norway, in April 2017 was entitled »Dialogue Pedagogy and Dialogue Method – What are the requirements of dialogue to our teaching and training of church workers?« (Dialogue Pedagogy and Dialogue Method – hvilke utfordringer stiller dialogen til vår undervisning og til utdannelsen av kirkelige medarbeidere?). A keynote analyzed the academic employment of these issues at the VID Vitenskapelige Høgskole Stavanger, the former Mission Highschool, including practical aspects of dialogue and pedagogy in Stavanger.

In October 2018 the conference moved again to Denmark, to Gentofte, a suburb north of Copenhagen, with the theme »Rituals and religious encounters – when the encounter of religions finds its way into the church« (Ritualer og Religionsmøde – når religionsmøder flytter ind i kirkerummet). This theme tackled the question how the pluralization of the religious landscape could affect the official services and the acting of the church. The following presentation and analysis in Section 4 takes up three church

---

[52] The main lecture by Oddbjørn Leirvik, Oslo, under the title »Luthersk teologi i mött med andra religioner« (Lutheran theology meeting other religions) can be found in a German translation (by Martin Affolderbach) in: Eißler, Friedmann / Funkschmidt, Kai (ed.), Religious Theology in the footsteps of Luther, EZW-Texts 250, Berlin 2017, pp. 29–41.

documents from Denmark, Norway and Sweden that addressed this question and played a central role in this meeting. These documents will be studied and taken up as an example to outline the nature of the discussion in these countries.

These Nordic meetings, which were consistently attended by around 30 to 60 participants and continued in Malmö, Sweden, in February 2020 under the title »The power and responsibility of majority churches in interfaith relations« address the inter-religious challenges from the perspective of the Lutheran People's Churches. Neither the Catholic Church nor the Orthodox Church nor free churches have been involved so far. Finland – despite one conference held in Helsinki – and Iceland were poorly represented, which undoubtedly has to do with the above-described religion-demographic situation and the consequently lower significance of inter-religious questions to these countries. The outlined development of the topics from very general problem formulations to more specific questions can certainly be interpreted as a serious and major concern that affects the churches in conceptional as well as in practical dimensions.

4. Church official services in a multi-religious society

Drawing on three documents from Denmark, Norway and Sweden, this section will now analyze how the Nordic Church reacted to the social changes with regard to their official services like baptism, weddings and funerals; how they analyzed the situation and what theological and practical consequences they drew from it.[53]

---

[53] A comparable German document is the elaboration by the Protestant Church in Germany (EKD), Öffentliche Trauerfeiern für Menschen unterschiedlicher Religionsgemeinschaften (Public funeral services for people from different religious communities), drafted by Christian Binder, Folkert Fendler, Stephan Goldschmidt and Wolfgang Reinbold; Hildesheim; published by the Zentrum für Qualitätsentwicklung im Gottesdienst (Center for Quality Development in Worship) in 2016. This document, which was prompted by the issue of funeral services in the field of military pastoral care, draws a very detailed picture of spiritual funeral services dependent on the degree and status of co-operation with a corresponding religious partner organisation, the religious identity and character of the deceased individual, and the respective mourning community.

4.1 Sweden – trans-boundary, but not without borders

An official position statement on the role of ecclesiastical official services in the plural society in Sweden, in particular baptisms, weddings and funerals, was published in 2012 as a Letter of the Lutheran Bishops[54]. Twenty years ago a handbook on the same topic had already been published[55]. The reason given for the renewed elaboration is that the meaning and the importance of the church's official services are less and less known to the public and especially to Christians in distance to the church and non-Christians. Official church services are strongly connected with feelings, so that especially these services including families of different faith traditions require a particularly careful preparation and respective accompaniment.

With regard to the demographic development, the Letter of the Bishops outlines that the Lutheran Church has hardly benefited from immigration, in contrast to smaller churches and other religious communities originating outside Sweden. People's identities often include different cultures, values or dual-religious identities. The legal status of migrants is sometimes uncertain. New communities have in instances taken over churches and buildings of the Swedish church and worship services are sometimes celebrated in several languages. Some migrants like to seek church help. The Swedish church is still an important representative of Swedish culture, which today is strongly secularized. Christian identities are very individualized, so that there is often a lack of knowledge and awareness of what unites with others faiths or what separates.

The overarching theological and pastoral idea understands the identity of the people's church as living in dialogue with people. In a multi-religious society this means (1) respecting others, (2) seeking links to other faith communities, and (3) finding a thoughtful theological attitude towards other communities. God's proximity in ecclesial ministry means to convey a sensitivity for the people involved, but also to interpret the meaning of a Christian ministry. The ten rules of thumb for good ecumenism[56] devel-

---

[54] De kyrkliga handlingarna i en mångreligiös kontext. Ett brev från Svenska kyrkans biskopar, Uppsala 2012.
[55] De kyrkliga handlingarna i mötet med invandrare. Ett pastoralt brev från Svenska kyrkans biskopar, Uppsala 1992.
[56] The document »Ten rules of thumb for a good Ecumenism« (Tio tumregler för god ekumenik) is available on www.skr.org/material (in Swedish).

oped by the Swedish Christian Council are important guidelines. There is no contradiction between a testimony for one's own faith and a dialogue. Conversion is not a goal, but every conversation should also provide explanation about one's own convictions. A good relationship with other faith communities is an important prerequisite for church ministries where different believers are involved. With regard to a well-considered religious-theological basic attitude, reference is made to a corresponding manual[57] which favours an inclusive understanding. Other religions can also be a place where the »Holy Spirit can dwell«. God's blessing includes also to other beliefs.

Many people have a mixed religious identity, which seems unproblematic to them. The Swedish Church has so far not developed a binding position on this, so that in each case it must be clarified in mutual talks with those concerned how one can deal with religious identity. There is in general no reason to exclude people. With regard to the question of a common prayer the bishops state with reference to other church handouts that other individuals can participate in prayers as guests. This would mean, that in official services discussed here, it is recommendable to say prayers »side by side«. In this context, a prayer »in Jesus' name« by the Christian part is possible. It is different with prayers which are carried out together, as these would presuppose a common conviction of faith. For the assessment of difficult constellations that can reoccur in this area, three criteria for good pastoral behaviour are given as guidelines:

1) The *consistency criterion:* The commandment of love should be taken as a yardstick for responsible decisions.
2) The *confessional criterion:* The Christian confession should be observed.
3) The *ecumenical criterion:* ll decisions should be considered in the light of inner-Christian, i.e. interdenominational, co-operation.

The bishops understand the baptism, an initiation rite and a sacrament of the Lutheran Church, as a sign of communion with God. If God is understood as the Creator of all human beings, non-Christians should be able to understand that baptism will contribute to a renewed life in service to

---

[57] Truly against yourself – open to others. Debate in the Swedish Church on theology of religion (Sann mot sig sjäv – öppen mot andra. Samtal om religionsteologi i Svenska kyrkan); see the Swedish version on www.svenskakyrkan.se/stockholmsstift.

God's kingdom and the welfare of all. With regard to baptisms, preparatory conversation should clarify whether the prerequisites are met and whether the participants have a mutual understanding of baptism. This is particularly important for persons who do not belong to the Lutheran Church. It should also be observed that the blessing of children has a different meaning. For the baptism of converts, asylum seekers and people without residence status, the Bishops point out that a baptism carried out in the target country cannot be claimed as a ground for asylum.

The confirmation as verification of the baptism is intended to support young people to become truly open to themselves and to others. In strongly multi-religious environments, co-operation with schools and other religious communities should be sought in order to explain the objectives of lessons on life and ethics for young people of this age and, if necessary, to cooperate. Whether young people with a non-Lutheran background can celebrate the confirmation must be examined on a case-by-case basis. Legal issues such as the provisions of the International Convention on the Rights of the Child should also be considered.

To the extent that the existing church orders are taken into account for marriage ceremonies, the Bishops do not believe that there are any concerns if a partner is not a church member. In the case of different denominations or religions, a conversation must clarify numerous questions and prerequisites: for example, the order of a possibly ecumenical or bi-religious worship service, involvements and responsibilities. Particularly in the case of the participation of Muslim spouses, legal questions also need to be clarified.

With regard to funerals, according to the Bishops, the religions differ with regard to their eschatology. While the Abrahamic religions have some convictions in common, the idea of reincarnation, for example, is not compatible with the Christian faith. Also not all religions practise a pastoral company in the case of death. In the case that funeral services are desired for persons who themselves or whose family members do not belong to the Lutheran Church or another Christian denomination or congregation, the three criteria mentioned above could provide assistance for decisions. However, in special cases of doubt, the governing bodies should be involved in decision-making.

Finally, the document emphasizes that the church's services are marked by concern for people and are therefore trans-boundary, but not without borders. The Christian faith and the church orders are in all cases the points of reference.

4.2 Norway – new challenges in a familiar environment

The Norwegian Bishops' guide to religious encounters in official church services[58] also starts from the position that over the past decades a religiously and culturally pluralistic society developed which has affected church life. Clergies and other church representatives need orientation when taking decisions on the numerous and difficult problems caused by those changes. However, this guideline concentrates on the relationship to the traditional world religions.

As in the Swedish handbook, the theological basis for the religious encounter is based on God's act of creation, which refers to the whole of humanity. The Bishops explain that there are numerous biblical thoughts and stories describing an exchange beyond religious borders: the story of creation, God's covenant with Abraham, the behaviour of Jesus towards others as a role model, Paul's speech on the Areopagus and the Logos teaching of the Gospel of John. The limits that Paul, for example, recommends to the congregation in Corinth in relation to idolatry do not suggest to reduce contact with people of other faiths should be avoided. The story of the Good Samaritan is an example of the universality of charity and goodness. As a summary of this biblical-theological analysis, the bishops present a Trinitarian text based on the Christian Creed which concisely formulates the biblical-theological insights mentioned and places them in a comprehensible context. The basic idea is that the message of the Gospel reaffirms and reinforces what God has revealed in wisdom through his Spirit.

Prayer plays a special role in religious encounters according to the assessment of the bishops. One possibility is, without any doubt, that Chris-

---

[58] Religionsmøtet ved kirkelige handlinger. En veiledning fra Bispemøtet, Oslo 2016; the document can be found (as pdf-file) on: www.kirken.no/globalassets; the Synod of the Lutheran Church debated on the topic »Religious Encounter and Dialogue« in April 2016 (www.kirken.no/nb-NO); in the Bishop's Council, the topic »Islam in Norway 2018« was on the agenda in February 2018 (www.kirken.no/nb-NO).

tians can be together with people of other religious convictions in silence or meditation. But the situation is different with regard to public prayers in a liturgical context. One form is the simple presence at the prayer of others. A second form are the prayers in which one prays side by side and each one in his tradition and responsibility, comparable to the Pope's peace prayer of 1986 in Assisi. In this context, a church participation should be responsibly weighed up in order to avoid possible misunderstandings. A third possibility is an »interreligious prayer«, i.e. the common speaking of an agreed text. According to the bishops, this is problematic above all with regard to the different ideas of God and not possible on the Christian side in public church services or in official acts. In principle, these assessments would also apply to private prayers.

In the case where people of other faiths ask Christian pastors for a pastoral conversation, they should make themselves available. Usually, however, the mediation of a corresponding person from the respective religion is advisable. According to the Bishops, the impression that in such situations an advantage is taken from the role of a majority church should be avoided, especially in public spaces such as hospitals. If pastoral conversations take place with people of Jewish or Muslim faith, texts could be helpful that are identical or similar in the Holy Scriptures of Judaism, Christianity and Islam.

Concerning the inter-religious encounters at the occasion of church services, the Bishops state in the third part of the document that baptism, confirmation, marriage and burial are among the rites that mark important transitions in human life in all cultures, but in different forms. In such rituals, the Christian faith and the Christian understanding of life are characterized by the confession of the triune God. The church building as a place of such services has its special character and its unique purpose. The guidelines how to use church rooms are set out in the respective rules of the Norwegian Church. At the same time the bishops emphasize that a church room should also be open to general human reflections and to meditation of beauty, life experience and wisdom which is in line with the basics of a theology of creation explained in the document.

With regard to marriages and burials the authors state that the prayers and liturgical texts are fixed and cannot simply be replaced by other religious texts or wording. However, in the case of the participation of different believers, there is the possibility to include other texts or pieces of music with intent which respect the character of the church room, the liturgical setting and do not contradict the church confession. With regard to the role of texts, music and dance from other traditions, it may be difficult to distinguish whether these can stand alone or be understood as separate liturgical acts. In order to avoid misunderstandings, it may be advisable in some cases that the person presiding over the worship service or an official act embeds and explains such pieces appropriately. Especially prayers from other religious traditions should be checked responsibly as to content and liturgical form as part of a Christian worship service without being misleading. According to the Bishops, spiritual actions of other religions cannot take place in a church building and must be separate from the corresponding church agenda. Also joint inter-religious services and official acts are not possible within the framework of the Norwegian Church. In the case of funerals which take place outside the church room itself, this has to be judged differently.

Baptism as a sacrament does mean not only participation in God's grace but also the formal admission into the Norwegian Church. Therefore, the act of baptism does not offer any possibility to include other religious elements. Especially in the case of bi-religious families, the preconditions for baptism have to be clarified. In exceptional cases, an act of intercession, prayer or blessing would be appropriate in order to decide on a baptism at a later point in time, for example, after the child or adolescent has reached religious maturity. Confirmation and preparatory lessons are closely linked to baptism and presuppose it. Members of other religions are, of course, free to attend a confirmation service. Participation in the Lord's Supper presupposes baptism. An exception could be made if a person could not be baptized due to life-threatening circumstances.

According to the bishops, school worship services have their own form, as both church and school are involved and teachers as well as pupils can participate. Nevertheless, the above principles also apply to such worship services. Persons from other faith traditions can participate as guests or, where necessary, contribute by reading texts.

Finally, under the heading »New challenges in a familiar environment«, the Bishops summarize that, since the historical beginnings, Christians have lived together in their families also with people of other convictions.

Therefore today, both openness as well as willingness to dialogue with others must go hand in hand with a clear commitment to one's own belief. This also contributes to a society which is characterized by enriching life understandings and faiths which are rooted in deeper convictions.

4.3 Denmark – Church services as rituals

For Denmark, the analyses is based on the »Report of the Project Group on Ecclesiastical Activities in a Society with Different Religions and World-views«, prepared by a project group of the Danish Churches' Office »People's church and religious encounter« (Folkekirke og Religionsmøde)[59]. Here, too, the starting point is the situation of a religiously pluralistic society, which places new demands on church action, as again and again non-Christians are involved in church services and actions in different ways. The document is intended to offer orientation and training assistance both for the clergymen at the local level as well as for professional education and further training.

The report begins by presenting some current religion-demographic data. Such data have already been presented above under section 1.1. With regard to residents with a migration background, it is stated that almost 13 percent are migrants from around 200 countries or their descendants. The largest groups stem from Turkey, Poland, Germany and Iraq, in that order. According to one study, marriages between ethnic Danes and people from non-Western cultural backgrounds pose a higher risk of divorce.[60]

The contributions of the report shed light on interreligious challenges in different social contexts. First, local congregations are described with a significant proportion of people of different religious or world views (see article 4.1[61]). A second contribution (4.2) focuses on the family and underlines the role of rituals and symbols in the context of marriages and life partnerships. A third section (4.3) focused on hospitals and therapies pre-

---

[59]   Tænketanke om kirkelige handlinger i et samfund med forskellige religioner og livssyn, Frederiksberg, 2016.
[60]   As a source, reference is made to an – not cited – investigation of the Rockwoll Fonden, Copenhagen (Rapport, op. Cit., p. 12). This private organization, founded in 1991, sees itself as independent and impartial and conducts studies on social and economic development in Denmark, including issues on social integration.
[61]   In the report, the numbers of the single articles are not in numerical order.

sents the experiences people have in physically and psychologically difficult situations with forms of silence and possibilities of conversation and reflection. The text tries to explore in which ways those rituals can help to rediscover the meaning of gratitude and forgiveness.

The role of rituals is examined sociologically in section 5.1: Historically, rituals have primarily served to legitimize institutions. In today's differentiated society, however, it is necessary to develop ritual creativity. For example, it is suggested that new rituals could be developed and tested within one's own four walls in order to create spaces for the exchange between people of different convictions.

The theological contribution to rituals in section 5.2 brings into consciousness the multitude of rituals that are compiled in the church agenda. The Danish name of this agenda, »Ritualbog«, already contains this keyword. This compilation should ensure a uniform and authorized application. The concept of rituals is not specifically defined in this article, but it is stated that ecclesiastical rituals are theologically assigned to the third article of the Creed, as they are related to God's presence by the Holy Spirit. Rituals would often include the blessing of God. In Lutheran doctrinal understanding, however, rituals are counted among the so-called adiaphora, i.e. those things which are not necessary for salvation and can be judged theologically and ethically differently. However, they have to serve the proclamation and arre thus assigned to preaching of the gospel. God's grace is not bound to anything; therefore God could also bring about new life through a ritual. Rituals are not simply everyday life, but are precisely in tension with it. They can symbolize the movement from old to new, from death to life or from loneliness to community, as church services and actions do.

After some explications concerning different situations in the everyday life of a multi-religious where rituals have their place today, the role of rituals is illuminated in a psychological sketch (section 6.1). People are controlled by values and feelings that are partly unconscious and deeply anchored. During life transitions and crises these could play a special role, but could also help to reorganize everyday life or attitudes and sensitivities. Couples with different religious backgrounds, especially those with strong beliefs and low tolerance toward those people who think differently, may be exposed to particular tensions and demands. In such constellations, both close friends and clergy could be helpful interlocutors to overcome crises through conversation and awareness of feelings. Church congregations could also play a helpful role.

In hospitals (contribution 6.2), »situational religiosity« can often occur independently of religious ties. According to a cited study a high percentage of patients pray, women significantly more than men (80 to 57 percent). Rituals such as a baptism could unfold a symbolic power especially in situations of illness.

A further contribution (7.1) examines the question of how pastors can adequately »administer« rituals in problematic inter-religious settings. The answer is that rituals are not part of everyday life, but stand in contrast and contradiction to it. Rituals and individualism stand in tension with each other.

In the concluding recommendations of the project group (section 8), the group does not see itself in a position to present a complete handbook, but proposes to address central questions:

1) by developing a course of action for pastors on rituals in the people's church[62],
2) through a conference of experts working towards a handbook for clergy and congregations, as well as
3) by developing study material for education and training purposes.

It remains to be seen, whether a document comparable to the Swedish and Norwegian documents will be produced. The above mentioned different social role of the Danish Bishops makes this probably rather unlikely, although the Danish church certainly has alternative possibilities at its disposal.

5. Cultural memory and openness for dialogue – a summary

The changes presented in the first part, show a continuous development in the Nordic countries over the past decades from a society which was, in

---

[62] Cf. also the document: Rapport fra Tænketanke vedr. Udredning og anbefalinger om religionsmøedekvalifikationer i fremtidens uddannelsesforløeb for præster in folkekirken, Frederiksberg 2015.

many respects, relatively uniform in terms of religion and culture, with the Lutheran churches as previous national churches, to multicultural and religiously plural societies. The centuries-old self-evident identity of being Danish, Finnish, Icelandic, Norwegian or Swedish and at the same time Lutheran Christian is quite obviously dissolving.

Although the core of these developments clearly points into the same direction in all Scandinavian countries, the underlying factors are very complex and multi-dimensional. Demographic change due to immigration is the most obvious and easiest to describe social developments. Changes in values, cultural patterns and everyday norms are much more difficult to map and analyse and often only manifest themselves in their consequences. The transformation of the relationship between state and church, as it was carried out in Sweden and Norway, exemplifies such a change below the surface, which entails the renewal of legal and structural social regulations and conventions. Even though such a separation has not yet taken place in Denmark, it is clear that many actors are aware of the changed social context. Therefore Denmark can be included when summarizing that in the Nordic churches a paradigm shift is taking place from a church majority culture - and the associated monopoly position of the Lutheran churches – towards a religiously and ideologically plural society as clearly recognized in the documents presented here.

The statistics of affiliations are only one dimension. Behind the numbers a mental change of the role of religion in society is taking place, which can be described in key words by the two terms individualization and secularization. Viggo Mortensen sums this up well when saying: »*People believe without belonging. This development co-exists in the Nordic countries with a parallel tendency of belonging without believing.*«[63]

The special constellation therefore consists of two aspects. On the one hand, besides the majority churches other religious communities of similar organisational structure join in. On the other hand, religious and ideological groups organise themselves very differently or even not at all. The frequent absence of definable counterparts and individually composed convictions mean that appropriate solutions can often only be found in the

---

[63] Mortensen, Viggo, Mapping, Analyzing and Interpreting Religious Pluralizm in Denmark, Europe and Beyond, in: Mortensen, Viggo, (Hrsg.), op. cit. (footnote 27), p. 56. The phrase and the meaning of »Believing without Belonging« was obviously first used by the American sociologist of religion, Grace Davie, in 1994.

individual case or through talks with people involved. The diversity of frequently individually different convictions and imprints hardly permits standardised solutions. The »new confusion« of beliefs is not only to be found in the space of other religions and world views, but also among those who formally belong to the churches.[64]

The conceptual reaction of the churches to this development is clearly recognizable: They prefer a double strategy of openness and dialogue on the one hand and an emphasis and clarification of one's own identity on the other hand.[65] Mogen S. Mogensen describes this vividly in an analogy:

> »An actor in the religious dialogue can be compared with a tree. The deeper the roots of a tree, the longer the crown can extend its branches without the tree falling down in a storm. Same with the members of the people's church who engage themselves in the religious dialogue: The more strongly they are rooted in the tradition of the church, its rituals, spirituality and doctrine, the further they can accommodate followers of other religions, understand them and also cooperate with them without losing their Christian identity.«[66]

It is remarkable in which way in particular the Norwegian document reflects and substantiates this conception in theological terms. It does not limit itself to a reference to God's action of creation only in order to achieve an inclusive understanding of faith and religion, but the document also traces the lines to stories of the Bible where the crossing of borders and dialogical situations can be identified. Thus the dimensions of Christian faith and religious and theological reflection come into view, which lead to a comprehensive understanding of being human and life, God and world and the points of contact to wisdom, religion and faith. Within such a framework the specifically Christian – and in this case even more pointedly: the Protestant-Lutheran – convictions of faith can then be placed. By

---

[64]   Viggo Mortensen sees above all a large number of people in search (»seekers«), who are therefore not defined in their beliefs. »Coming out of a situation where one religion held almost a monopoly position, the church has a great problem in developing a religious supply that can meet the spiritual demand in a changing cultural situation. The people develop their own religious doctrines and rituals.« (ibid., p. 52).

[65]   In this article it must be disregarded that there are also other positions within the churches on this issue. Especially groups that are critical of Islam or those for whom Christian mission is important are critical of a dialogue-oriented approach. For Denmark see: Lulu Hjarnø, Fremdenfeindlichkeit und Islamphobie in Dänemark (Xenophobia and Islamophobia in Denmark), in: Micksch, Jürgen / Schwier, Anja, Islam in europäischen Dörfern (Islam in European villages), Frankfurt/Main, 2002, pp. 77–84.

[66]   Mogensen, Mogen S., op.cit. (footnote 27), p. 13.

offering answers to basic human questions, these convictions in turn are open to dialogue and thus dialogical in their structure.

This concept understands the religiously and ideologically pluralistic situation not as a religious market on which one wants to praise and »sell« one's own »product« with unique selling points and in competition to other offers, but as a communicative and inclusive understanding of community. Universal human commonalities as starting point do not demarcate or defend hostile counterparts, but underline a comprehensive common framework. Thus, this approach is in a new sense »people's church« oriented and not aimed at shaping a minority identity that is defined by boundaries.

The basic political direction of understanding oneself as a multicultural society – at least in Sweden –, intends to prevent social segregation and to keep the promise of a democratically pluralistic society that aims for peace and well-being through the integration and participation of as many groups as possible. The churches have not only undertaken efforts to develop a new position, but they are also active discussants and actors in this process.

Jenny Berglund observed processes of adaptation of Muslim minorities in Sweden to the new social situation.[67] Her study on the teaching of Islamic religion in selected schools shows the efforts towards a concept of »glocalization«. This concept tries to connect the traditional offers of interpretation of Islam with the challenges of a modern Swedish society as well as those of globalization, when dealing with the question of authentic Islam. It highlights how the influence of tradition, the local school context, the current environment and the issues discussed at the global level are interwoven.[68]

The three documents demonstrate that the churches are responding to the new framework conditions, want to explain their official actions to the general public and open up to dialogue. Putting a spotlight on church services and ministries as »rituals« does not, however, lead to completely new rituals being considered or included, although one essay recommends ritual creativity. In this sense it is correct and consistent that one's own identity should be underlined and made more recognizable. But this

---

[67] See above footnote 18.
[68] See the summary in Berglund, Jenny, op.cit. (footnote 18), p. 204f.

should not lead to a boundless openness for any religious ritual. Rather, they need to be examined as to their authenticity, theological coherence and not just a response to short-term trends.

The Scandinavian churches can certainly preserve their authenticity and develop it further if they continue to fulfil their role as collective religious tradition and cultural memory. This could be achieved by continuing to preserve their distinct Scandinavian or national imprint not in museum-like rigidity but through critical openness. Furthermore, there is also a need to rethink contemporary challenges in theological terms and introduce new ideas and visions into society applying participatory openness and professional quality.

Inter-religious Co-operation in Europe

The example of the European Council of Religious Leaders

The social changes that have taken place in recent decades towards a multicultural and multi-religious society affect virtually all countries in Europe. In addition to numerous contacts, dialogues and cooperations between different religious communities at local, regional and national levels, there have also been efforts to organise and intensify cooperation and exchange at the European level. Responses to such historically new challenges are often initiated and driven by individuals before they are taken over by existing organisations or before they become institutionalized. This similarly applies to the initiative presented here in this article, namely the European Council of Religious Leaders (ECRL).

In the context of this article, it is not possible to provide a complete review of the Council's entire work.[1] Rather, the aim is to provide an overview of some selected events, themes and policy concepts to illustrate the Council's intention to establish itself, its objectives, its activities and projects and its role in the European context.[2]

The following presentation is thus divided into a section on the creation and working structure of the Council, followed by a section on the topics and the strategic priorities. The third section takes a look at the European

[1] The following is based on self-portrayals of ECRL, published statements, annual reports and other documents, which, for reasons of clarity and readability, are mentioned here in total. Individual references are included where necessary. All internet sources were last accessed in August 2019.

[2] I would like to thank Bishop em. Prof. Dr. Martin Hein, Kassel, Bishop em. Gunnar Stålsett, Oslo, Jehangir Sarosh, London, and the ECRL office at the University of Winchester, United Kingdom, namely Rebecca Bellamy and Dr. Marc Owen, for information and useful assessments.

embedding of ECRL, followed by a brief review and outlook in the last part.

1. The origin and working structure of the Council

The impetus for the creation of a European Council of senior representative figures from religious communities came from leading members of Religions for Peace at the European and international level[3], notably Bill Vendley[4], Religions for Peace International, New York, and Jehangir Sarosh[5], Religions for Peace Europe, London. In addition to the structure of Religions for Peace, which consist of local groups and individuals engaged in interreligious dialogue, most of whom are volunteers, the need for a new body at the European level was identified. This group should be composed of leading figures from the religious communities in Europe to profit from their experiences, reputation and authority.

Bishop Gunnar Stålsett[6], at that time Bishop of Oslo and leading bishop of the Norwegian (Lutheran) Church, took up this suggestion in 2001 and invited some leading figures to a meeting in Paris. This gathering was attended by eight representatives from the Abrahamic religions: including Bishop Stålsett as host, Grand Rabbin René-Samuel Sirat from Paris, the Grand Mufti of Bosnia-Herzegovina Mustafa Cerić from Sarajevo, Metropolitan Kyrill of Smolensk and Kaliningrad[7] from Russia and Godfried Cardinal Daneels, Archbishop of Mechelen-Brussels.

---

[3] More information on »Religions for Peace«, which held its 10th World Assembly for the first time in Germany at the end of August 2019 in Lindau at Lake Constance, can be found in particular on the relevant websites of Religions for Peace International (www.rfp.org), Religions for Peace Europe (www.religionsforpeace.net and www.ecrl.eu) and Religions for Peace Germany (www.religionsforpeace.de).

[4] Dr. William F. Vendley was the Secretary General of Religions for Peace international from 1994 to 2019.

[5] Jehangir Sarosh was the President of Religions for Peace Europe for ten years.

[6] Gunnar Stålsett, born 1935 in the far north of Norway, was a leader in politics as well as the church. After serving as Secretary of State for Church Affairs and Education (1972–1973), he was a member of the Norwegian Parliament (1977 to 1981) and from 1977 to 1979 chaired the Norwegian Centre Party. After working as a pastor and university lecturer at the University of Oslo, he became General Secretary of the Lutheran World Federation from 1985 to 1993, Bishop of Oslo from 1998 to 2005 and leading Bishop of the Norwegian Church. After leaving the episcopal residence, he continues to work internationally for various projects.

[7] Since 2009 as Cyril I Patriarch of Moscow and All Russia.

This group agreed that such a body should not be composed in proportion to the size of the respective religious communities, but should consist of a council of 30 persons with five official representatives from six religious or denominational groups each, namely Catholicism, Protestantism, Orthodoxy, Judaism, Islam and other religions. Such leaders should be addressed by personal contact. Each of these religious groups should be asked to propose a representative for the role of a co-moderator of the Council. The ex officio membership of Bill Vendley and Jehangor Sarosh strengthened the link with Religions for Peace to consciously establish the European Council of Religious Leaders as a complementary institution rather than a replacement to the existing structures of Religions for Peace Europe.

The official constitution of ECRL took place in 2002 in the episcopal residence of Bishop Stålsett in Oslo. On this occasion, the Norwegian Foreign Minister welcomed this foundation in his speech and declared it as a necessary step worthy of support. declared it as a necessary step worth supporting. Bishop Stålsett, together with the co-moderators, took over the leadership of the committee and, with the financial support of Norwegian Church Aid[8], set up a secretariat for ECRL in Oslo.

Shortly thereafter, the Norwegian Ministry of Foreign Affairs supported the work with a grant of 2 million Norwegian crowns[9] to finance annual meetings of the Council and further planned activities. Contacts were also established with the World Council of Churches and the Lutheran World Federation and invitations were issued for representatives of these organisations to the respective meetings. The Council endeavoured to expand the circle of members as soon as possible, especially beyond the Abrahamic religions, and to try hard to achieve more complete representation from religious communities in Europe.

Concerning the format of the meetings, each meeting had a defined theme of particular interest to the religious communities, which promoted the cooperation of the religious communities in Europe and contributed to a peaceful development. For example, the issues of religious freedom and the problems of anti-Semitism and xenophobia were among the

---

[8] Norwegian Church Aid (Norwegian: Kirkens Nødhjelp) is an independent aid organization that works in close collaboration with the Norwegian Lutheran Church.
[9] According to the market value at that time about 267.000 €.

themes of the early years. At most of the meetings, public statements or declarations were adopted on the topics dealt with,[10] for example, in the first period of the Council's work statements on tolerance, a plea for a culture of peace and on the issue of anti-Semitism.

In addition to the Council itself, an Executive Committee was entrusted with advising the administration on day-to-day issues and with preparing the meetings of the Council. In 2007 it was agreed that the members of the Executive Committee could be represented by a substitute if they were unable to attend.

It became possible to establish a full-time office for the Council, temporarily with three specialists. From 2006 to 2010, Vebjørn L Horsfjord was the Secretary General of the Council. From 2011 to 2014 he was succeeded in this function by Stein Villumstad, who had previously been Deputy Secretary General of Religions for Peace International in New York for five years. Starting in 2007, Ingrid Rosendorf Joys took over the Council's public relations work for several years. Since 2012 Thomas Wipf[11] – succeeding Bishop Stålsett – serves as moderator of ECRL.

Since most of the Council's financial resources[12] were provided by Norwegian donors, most notably by the Ministry of Foreign Affairs, it became very urgent from 2012 onward to look for new funding opportunities. As the Ministry changed its priorities in the area of development cooperation and special funds for Syria, the funding for ECRL ran out at the end of 2013. As it was very difficult to find new sources, Jehangir Sarosh in London took over the administration of the Council on a temporary basis.

After internal consultations on a restructuring of ECRL, a consultation process with the members and partners of the Council was conducted in 2016 under the auspices of the University of Wincester and an »Agenda for Change – To think and act together« was submitted for consultation in 2017. It acknowledged the Council's good potential, but also recommended to explore a new culture of cooperation, to strive for broader regional rep-

---

[10]　More on this in the next section below.

[11]　From 1999 to 2010 Thomas Wipf was the President of the Council of the Swiss Confederation of Churches and in this function from 2004 to 2010 he was also a member of the Praesidium of the Conference of European Churches (CEC). He founded the Swiss Council of Religions in 2006 and was its President until 2010. During the same period, he also served as President of the Community of Evangelical Churches in Europe (CPCE).

[12]　The financial contributions from the members of the Council has always been very low. In 2012, only four members are said to have contributed financially.

resentation, to increase the proportion of women, to improve the financial situation and to seek closer contact to European institutions in Brussels. Internally, the main objectives were to make participation and financial support by members more binding and strengthen the transmission of the work of ECRL into the respective religious communities. With regard to better external relations, the predominant desire was to anchor the Council more strongly in the field of European institutions and to create a more solid financial security for its work. The relocation of the office from Oslo to Brussels was a wish, but the possibilities to implement such move were missing.[13]

With regard to the management, a solution was found. Contacts with Dr Mark Owen, Centre of Religion Reconciliation and Peace at the University of Winchester, England, led to a corresponding agreement in 2016, so that he assumed the function of Secretary General in 2017.

The Council currently counts 44 members[14], five of whom are Jews, five from the Catholic Church, five from the Protestant and Anglican Churches, three from the Orthodox Church, six Muslim representatives and five from the Eastern religions of Buddhism, Hinduism, Sikh and Zoroastrian (»Dharmic religions«[15]). There are also six consultants and ex-officio members, including Gunnar Stålsett. Eight of the members are from Great Britain or Scotland, four from Germany, three from France, two from Italy and Switzerland each, one each from Belgium, Denmark, Finland, Greece, the Netherlands, Norway, Austria, Poland, Sweden, Slovenia and Hungary.

---

[13] ECRL was officially registered in Brussels as an organization under Belgian law (International non-profit Association (AISBL)) in 2018 with the intention to facilitate the establishment of a formal relationship with European institutions.

[14] State of the information August 2019. The current information as well as the names of the persons can be found on the ECRL homepage (www.ecrl.eu). However, in the 2019 annual report (text see www.ecrl.eu) the number of 32 members out of a possible 42 is given.

[15] »Dharmic religions« refers to religions that have arisen on the Indian subcontinent and that, based on certain common beliefs, are viewed as a family of religions.

2. Goals and guiding principles

The aim of ECRL foresees that the Council should

»form a coalition of religious leaders in Europe who have committed themselves to cooperate on conflict prevention and transformation, peaceful coexistence and reconciliation, and who encourage members of their communities to do the same«[16].

These objectives are set out in ECRL's self-presentation as follows:

»ECRL's guiding values and principles include adherence to a number of important ethical, moral and spiritual ideals and principles:
- The appreciation of religious diversity and diversity and the willingness to learn from other religions and beliefs.
- The willingness to identify common values and concerns, and the willingness to act together.
- The holiness of all creation and the lasting goal of achieving positive and sustainable peace.
- The willingness to defend and promote human dignity, human rights and the freedom of all religions and beliefs.«[17]

These goals have been constantly updated in the consultations of the Council and in regard to numerous topics and activities, and have on many occasions been linked to the respective occasions and settings. The slogan »Different Faiths – Common Action« has often been used to describe the specific nature of this cooperation.

2.1 Thematic priorities and public statements

The main topics of the Council's meetings and the public statements and declarations, which were quite often associated with the debate of a topic, provide an initial overview of the content of ECRL's work. The following outlines the main stages of the Council's work.

To the aforementioned official constitution of ECRL in Oslo in November 2002, representatives from the Christian denominations, Judaism, Islam, Baha'i and Zoroastrianism from Albania, Belgium, Bosnia-Herzegovina, France, Great Britain, Norway, Romania, Russia, Turkey, Hungary and the Vatican as well as representatives of Religions for Peace were in-

---

[16] Constitution of ECRL, I Basis, 14 February 2007.
[17] See leaflet of self-presentation at www.ecrl.eu.

vited. At that occasion, Bishop Stålsett stated that it was the Council's task to contribute to the dialogue between conflicting parties in conflict situations, to play an active role in promoting religious freedom in Europe and, as a multi-religious European voice, to make a responsible contribution to global dialogue. That is why a new form of inter-religious cooperation is necessary, especially under the impressions of the terrorist attacks of 11 September 2001. The declaration »Standing together for peace – The inauguration meeting of the ECRL«[18] summarises the intentions of the foundation.

The second meeting of the newly founded Council was held in Leuven, Belgium, in November 2002, and dealt with the conflict in the Balkans and published a statement on the situation in Sarajevo.[19] Members of the Council had visited the region in the previous month. The declared intention to seek moderation of talks with conflicting parties[20] was then implemented by holding separate talks with representatives from both Kosovo and Bosnia-Herzegovina in parallel with the Council meeting in Leuven, Belgium, from 7 to 10 November 2004. In addition, a Council statement on the current situation in Kosovo[21] was prepared and published, and a delegation from ECRL was scheduled to visit Kosovo.

A statement on the crisis caused by the Mohammed cartoons[22] was published by ECRL in February 2006. This document took up statements by the British and European Islamic Conferences in condemning violence and described the balance to be found between freedom of religious belief and freedom of expression.

A declaration entitled »Religions for peace – challenging terrorism and extremism«[23], adopted by the ECRL at its meeting from 12 to 14 February 2007 in the centre of the Sikh community Guru Nanak Nishkam Sewak Jatha in Birmingham, Great Britain, was strongly affected by the terrorist attacks of radical Muslims in those years, especially a serious attack in London. The text calls for further steps towards the integration of migrants,

---

[18] For the wording, see www.ecrl.eu.
[19] For the wording of the Sarajevo Declaration, see www.ecrl.eu.
[20] Such conversations with representatives of (religious) conflict parties behind closed doors are also conducted and organized by Religions for Peace International as so-called Track II talks, an important area of the organization's international peace work.
[21] For the wording, see www.ecrl.eu.
[22] The text of the »Statement on the Cartoon Crises« can be found on www.ecrl.eu.
[23] For the wording, see www.ecrl.eu.

an intensification of (religious) education and increased confidence-building among religious representatives. At this meeting, an official agreement on the cooperation of ECRL with Religions for Peace[24] International and Religions for Peace Europe, called »Memorandum of Understanding«, was adopted. As in previous years, those agreements have been deliberately kept open for additions and updates.

In October of the same year, the Executive Committee of ECRL met in Oslo and adopted a statement on the situation in Burma[25] condemning the military government's response to peaceful protests in the country, calling for talks with the democratic movement, religious communities, the ethnic groups and with the Burmese politician Aung San Suu Kyi who was an active peacekeeper at that time and received the 1991 Nobel Peace Prize. The worldwide appeal of Religions for Peace International to use the influence on all sides for a peaceful solution of the conflict was expressly welcomed and supported. In a further statement, the Open Letter from 138 Muslim representatives to all Christian churches[26], published only a few days before the meeting of the Executive Committee, was welcomed and appreciated. A Christian response to this letter should be used in a globally coordinated way to initiate a sustained dialogue and joint practical steps between Muslims and Christians. The ECRL offered its cooperation in this regard.[27]

During the annual meetings of the following years statements were elaborated and published, for example at the meeting of the Council in Berlin in March 2008, at the Council's visit to the Jewish synagogue in Berlin. A statement on the topic »Healing of memories and facing the future. The role of religion in the dialogue of cultures«[28] was adopted against the background of the »European Year of Interreligious Dialogue« in 2008 and mediation talks with representatives from the conflict regions of the Balkans. A declaration on »Total ban on cluster munitions – a moral responsibility«[29] was issued in October of the same year at a meeting in

---

[24]   At that time, the official name was still »World Conference of Religions for Peace« (WCRP).

[25]   For the wording, see www.ecrl.eu.

[26]   A Common Word Between Us and You, Amman/Jordan, October 13, 2007.

[27]   The wording of the opinion can be found at www.ecrl.eu. Vebjørn L Horsfjord, at that time General Secretary of ECRL evaluated the responses to the open letter in: Common Words in Muslim-Christian Dialogue: A Study of Texts from the Common Word Dialogue Process (Currents of Encounter, Brill, Volume 57), Leiden/Boston, 2017.

[28]   For the text of the statement, see www.ecrl.eu.

Sarajevo, following the invitation of the Interreligious Council of Bosnia-Herzegovina and also attended by other organisations.

At the February 2009 meeting in Lille, France, a »Declaration on a Culture of Peace«[30] was adopted, which is factually linked to the United Nations Decade to Promote a Culture of Peace (2001–2010). A year later, in 2010, at the Istanbul meeting, a statement on tolerance was published entitled »Our commitment to Justice, Equality and Sharing«. A report was also given on the five-year global campaign »Restoring Dignity – End Violence against Women Initiative«, which includes projects in numerous countries, particularly in Africa, Asia and Latin America, and which was supported by ECRL, Religions of Peace and other organisations. The statement »Arms Race Violates Religion, Culture of Peace, and Millennium Development Goals«[31] was adopted in October of that year by the Executive Committee at its meeting in London.

The Council meeting in Moscow in June 2011 issued a declaration on »Advancing Human Dignity – through human rights and traditional values«. The phrase »traditional values« needs to take into account the Russian context where – with the support of the Orthodox Church – certain reservations are held towards religious communities which have newly immigrated to the country or are demanding freedom for religious life in a Western understanding. Thus an exchange on the understanding of religious freedom was carried out and recorded in the declaration. The concern of the Russian side is recognizable under paragraph 7 when it says: »Traditional values are often deeply rooted and may in practice have greater authority in society than the positive right«. The »Universal Code on Holy Sites« was also presented at this meeting in Moscow, a document which was produced within three years by a co-operation between the Oslo Centre for Peace and Human Rights, the organization One World in Dialogue and Religions for Peace. This document lists a series of measures intended to protect sacred sites of religions and to initiate understanding in reference to conflict situations. It was published in January 2011, adopted by a num-

---

[29] For the text of the statement, see www.ecrl.eu.
[30] For the text of the statement, see www.ecrl.eu.
[31] For the text of the statement, see www.ecrl.eu.

ber of religious communities and organizations[32] and tested in a pilot project by the Council of Religious Leaders in Israel (CRLI) and Council of Religious Institutions of the Holy Land (CRIHL).

In May 2012, the meeting was held in Sarajevo, Bosnia-Herzegovina. The Sarajevo Declaration[33], which looks back on ten years of existence of ECRL, recalls commitments from previous statements and formulates nine theses on the vision of a supportive society that offers space for the development of the diversity of its members.

In May 2013, the next annual meeting took place in Vienna, Austria, in co-operation with the Organisation for Security and Cooperation in Europe (OSCE) and, in particular, its Office for Democratic Institutions and Human Rights (ODIHR) based in Warsaw. A Declaration on the Promotion of Religious Freedom was adopted. With reference to previous statements and to relevant international conventions on the subject the document concludes with a self-commitment:

»We commit ourselves to co-operate amongst ourselves and with other religious groups, governmental and inter-governmental institutions, in promoting understanding, respect and co-operation among all religious communities for the peace and well-being of all.«

In May 2015, the annual meeting of ECRL took place in Frankfurt am Main and discussed the problems of religious extremism as well as the future of the work. The participants underlined the importance to understanding the causes of religious fundamentalism and extremism in order to be able to take the appropriate targeted measures. The religious values of peace and minimization of violence must be the guiding principles. Together with Religions for Peace and other international organizations, an action plan was regarded as urgently needed to combat the abuse of religion.

The Council meeting in May 2016 in Brixen, Italy, was entitled »Refugee and migration situation in Europe – addressing potential for disharmony«

---

[32]   This initiative received current support through the establishment of a »Rings for Peace« at the World Assembly of RfP in Lindau in August 2019 (see www.ringforpeace.org) and a corresponding planned declaration by the Secretary General of the United Nations, for which a corresponding ring is also to be placed at the United Nations building in New York.

[33]   For the wording of the declaration »Ten Years of Living Together in Diversity and Harmony (Sarajevo Declaration)« see www.ecrl.eu.

and sum-marised the deliberations in the statement »Mass Migration: A European Challenge«. The conference also dealt with the Sustainable Development Goals adopted by the United Nations General Assembly in 2015 and the upcoming celebrations of 500 years of Reformation.

In May 2017, a meeting was held in Turku, Finland, to discuss, among others, the future of ERCL on the basis of the above-mentioned »Agenda for Change – To think and act together«, which, as mentioned above, evaluated a consultation process among members of the Council and its partners. The following May, the Council's annual meeting took place in Budapest, Hungary. As a result of the discussions, the »Budapest Statement on The Role of Multi-religious Cooperation in Social Cohesion and Human Security«[34] was published, calling on political and religious leaders and others to respect the human dignity of migrants and refugees and to avoid polemics and demagogy.

In March 2019, ECRL published a statement on the violence against two mosques in Christchurch, New Zealand. In August 2019 the World Assembly of Religions for Peace took place in Lindau, Germany[35]. ECRL contributed to this event through intensive preparation and collaboration.

2.2 Activities and projects

In addition to the topics and issues dealt with at the annual meetings of the Council – and in some cases also at meetings of the Executive Committee –, the ECRL engaged in several other activities. Numerous statements and calls required practical implementation by ECRL itself. In some years, comprehensive »strategy papers«[36] were drawn up and adopted. Some of the main points are listed below.

- The establishment of inter-religious councils (internal abbreviation: »IRCs«) in countries where they do not yet exist was a continuous task, as these councils were understood as national partners. This task was seen as particularly urgent in conflict regions. This was, for example,

---

[34] For the wording, see www.ecrl.eu.
[35] For more information on this conference, which was supported intensively by the »Ring for Peace« foundation, see www.ringforpeace.org.
[36] Such papers were presented as Work Plan 2007/2008, Action Plan 2012/2013 and Strategy Paper 2013–2018.

achieved in Kosovo, but, despite considerable efforts, not in the Caucasus region.

- Mediation in conflict situations is one of ECRL's remarkable activities, which not only included talks with conflict partners in Bosnia-Herzegovina and Kosovo, as mentioned above, but also outside Europe with those in Sri Lanka and East Timor. A moderation of talks in Kyrgyzstan in 2010 was met by criticism by the Orthodox Patriarchate in Moscow. Other projects, such as in Georgia, could not be realised due to limited funds. In this context conferences with conflict partners in Iraq, which took place in different places, should also be mentioned.
- ECRL has initiated a number of projects together with other agencies or supported those which were initiated by other agencies. These include, for example, the annual »Interfaith Harmony Week« initiated by Jordan and adopted by the United Nations General Assembly in 2010. ECRL also supported campaigns on »Banning Cluster Munitions« and on HIV and AIDS.
- Advisory meetings and conferences were a frequently used format, for which the cooperation with the relevant other partners was often sought. A European inter-religious conference on »Shared Values for a Changing Europe« in 2008 could be mentioned as an example.
- In the field of public relations, the development of a »European inter-religious directory« can be cited as one still ongoing activity.

With regard to the current projects and work plans, the following projects (as of 2019) should be mentioned, some of which have already been implemented:

1) In cooperation with the Institute of Democratic and Electoral Assistance (IDEA)[37], discussions are to be conducted and evaluated with religious representatives and their communities in Hungary, Germany, Ireland and Wales on their understanding of religious freedom under the topic »Religion and Constitution«.
2) The above-mentioned preparation and participation of ECRL at the 2019 World Conference in Lindau is a second project.

---

[37]   IDEA is an international organization for the promotion of democracy worldwide founded by 14 states in 1995 with headquarter in Stockholm (see www.idea.int).

3) A mapping of the interreligious activities of women and young people is to be drawn up, and

4) an interactive Internet platform on which successful projects on the topics of the World Conference, namely Transforming Conflict, Promoting Just and Harmonious Societies, Advancing Sustainable, Integral Human Development and Protecting the Earth can be accessed.[38]

5) In cooperation with the University of Wincester, projects on religion and migration in various European countries will be surveyed.[39]

6) Discussions will be held between religious representatives from the Middle East (MENA) and European countries on the challenges of migration between the two regions.[40]

ECRL has repeatedly advocated the empowerment of women and the participation of young people. There is close cooperation with the European Women of Faith Network, founded in Brussels in 2008, and the European Interfaith Youth Network (EIYN), established two years earlier. Both networks operate as independent structures within the framework of Religions for Peace[41]. ECRL seeks to further strengthen its cooperation with these networks.

3. European embeddedness

Since its foundation, ECRL has sought contact with European partners and institutions as well as cooperation with organisations pursuing similar objectives.

In the religious field, the close cooperation with the different levels of Religions for Peace, their women's and youth network, the national religious councils in various countries and the structures of the religious communities themselves as well as the Conference of European Churches, the European (Catholic) Bishops' Conference, the World Council of Chris-

---

[38] See also the homepage www.religions-in-action.eu.

[39] A report on this is available in the brochure »Multi-religious Approach to Integration«, published by ECRL and the University of Winchester, 2019.

[40] These were also the subject of the presentation at a plenary session of the world conference Religions for Peace in Lindau.

[41] More information can be found on www.ecrl.eu.

tian Churches, Muslim associations and the representations of other religious communities was a matter of course.

In order to be able to reach out to the societal space, contacts to the political structures in Europe are, of course, also of importance. ECRL has
an official status as partner organisation of the Council of Europe and
thus takes part in the annual exchange with the Council on interreligious
and intercultural questions. As mentioned above, contacts also exist with
the Organization for Security and Cooperation in Europe (OSCE) and its
Department for Democratic Institutions and Human Rights (ODIHR). In
addition, there are contacts and professional exchanges with the European
Parliament and the Commission of the European Union.

With regard to the European Union as one of the most important political actors in Europe, it can be noticed that, on the one hand, the Union
regards itself as a community of values and thus has a similar ethical
basis to that expressed by ECRL in its goals and themes, and, on the other
hand, shows the profile of a predominately economic community as a
result of its origins. In 1992, Jacques Delors, former President of the Commission of the European Union, introduced the position that »Europe
needs a soul«. This has led to a greater integration of religious and cultural
aspects into the work of the European Union.[42]

Commission President José Manuel Barroso already expressed his interest in a stronger integration of this social field into the work of the European Union at the beginning of his term of office in 2004. He invited
representatives of the religious communities to an annual exchange starting
2005. Religious communities were asked to nominate the appropriate persons for these meetings from their part. The Treaty of Lisbon, signed in
2007, takes this line further by stating that the EU intends »to maintain
an open, transparent and regular dialogue with churches and (religious
and non-confessional) communities in recognition of their identity and

---

[42] The call of Jacques Delors was initially addressed to the churches but also taken up by
other civil actors (cf. Hoburg, Ralf, Protestantismus und Europa, Berlin 1999, p. 14 and
89). A number of studies evaluating after 25 years how Delors' suggestion was taken up
and implemented see: van den Brink, Gijsbert / den Hertog, Gerard, (eds.), Protestant
Traditions and the Soul of Europe, Beihefte zur Ökumenischen Rundschau 110, Leipzig
2017.

specific contribution« (Article 17.3).[43] Consequently, ECRL has also maintained contact with the Commissioner for Dialogue with Churches, Religions and Non-Confessional Organisations of the European Commission and has offered itself as a contact group and a platform for dialogue between the European Union and religious communities.

The cooperation of ECRL with organisations and initiatives at the global scale such as the Alliance of Civilization or UNESCO is understandably used above all in cases when joint projects or initiatives are carried out.

4. Assessments and outlook

With regard to an evaluative assessment of ECRL's work, the first question that arises is whether the self-imposed goals have been implemented.

The intention to form a »coalition of leading religious representatives« has certainly been implemented and has also led to a sustainable and stable setting of institutional cooperation. ECRL seems to have found a place and a reputation in the European arena, which is undoubtedly mainly due to the commitment of some leading representatives. As mentioned above, some countries are more involved in the Council's work, a number of Eastern and Southern European countries show less interest. To strike an appropriate regional balance is certainly a task for the coming years.

Another question is whether the intention to bring in as many leaders in the Council as possible is really realistic. It is questionable whether in some areas representatives who do not have a direct leadership position but great expertise are needed and helpful. A leading role in the respective religious community might not be the exclusive criterion, rather the personal and convincing commitment to the goals of ECRL might be of importance. In addition, it is paramount to what extent a stronger commitment, regression and implementation of joint projects in the respective religious communities can be guaranteed by the respective persons. The formulation that the members of the Council commit themselves to en-

---

[43] Irmgard Schwaetzer, President of the Synod of the Evangelical Church in Germany (EKD), emphasizes in a lecture on the role of religions in Europe: »The EU recognizes the importance of religions as a dialogue partner for politics.« (Schwaetzer, Irmgard, Die Rolle der Religionen in Europa (The role of religions in Europe), March 2014; Source: www.ekd.de).

courage their communities to join the objectives of ECRL takes into account that in some parts of the religious communities such goals are not or only partly shared. In this respect, the goals of ECRL are an internal task and challenge for religious communities that should not be underestimated. In this sense, ECRL's activities have also an internal pedagogical function.

One main objective of ECRL's work is to »work together for the prevention and transformation of conflicts, for the promotion of peaceful coexistence and reconciliation«. The programme and the topics the Council has worked on in recent years demonstrate considerable implementations of these goals. The objective »prevention and transformation of conflicts« has been implemented by the moderation of talks with conflict parties, but also by declarations dealing with extremism, by comments on the cartoons crisis, by the Code for the Protection of Holy Places, by the Declaration on Burma and statements on the banning of cluster bombs and nuclear weapons. The keyword »promoting peaceful coexistence« is substantiated by the declarations and projects on the culture of dialogue and peace, violence against women, the Millennium Development Goals of the United Nations, religious freedom, social cohesion and the treatment of migrants and refugees. The term »reconciliation« is addressed in a specific way through the healing of memories.

Numerous declarations take the form of self-commitments or ambitious appeals, which are often difficult to assess as to whether they only had a declaratory effect or whether they could be implemented into practical action and concrete projects. There are no research or studies on this, but there are sporadic pointers in the annual reports of ECRL. In regard to practical implementation it is, of course, crucial to check whether the human and financial resources are available. Considering that ECRL has no secure financing, the available resources must be clarified for all projects.

The contact and cooperation with the European women's and youth networks may still offer opportunities that could be harnessed more strongly in the future, whereby the concentration on »senior religious leaders« by definition sets certain limits and raises the question of how the composition of the committee can be further developed.

It is apparent that ECRL and Religions for Peace Europe presents a certain duality. Against this background talks have taken place under the moderation of Religions for Peace International which concluded in agreement in spring 2019 that ECRL should play a leading role in coordinating and bringing together cooperation at the European level in the coming years. It is therefore to be expected that the Council will continue to play a pivotal role in the European inter-religious context in the coming years.

Religions as Civil Actors

Current global strategies for inter-religious co-operation

Religions for Peace (RfP), which considers itself to be the world's largest interfaith network[1], can look back on a history of 50 years in 2020. This is a suitable occasion to investigate the role of cooperation between representatives of different religious communities and religious beliefs in an increasingly globalised society. Which common goals and fields of action have been developed by the network and what effects and repercussions does this cooperation have on the religious communities themselves?

Religions for Peace is neither the only network that strives for interreligious cooperation worldwide, nor is it historically one of the first efforts in this field.

Efforts to cooperate between religions and projects for dialogue and understanding across religious boundaries have been made many times in human history.[2] Two aspects were the main drivers behind these ventures.

On the one hand, the objective was to minimise or pacify tensions and conflicts in a community with groups of different religious affiliations and to promote peaceful coexistence, something we now call the promotion of social peace and integration. As a historical example, the period from the 8th century onwards in Muslim Spain (al-Andalus) is often referred to

---

1   »*Religions for Peace* is the world's largest and most representative multi-religious coalition advancing common action for peace.« www.rfp.org/about/history (visited 3/2020; all visits to internet websites mentioned in this article took place in 3/2020).
2   Cf. Dehn, Ulrich, Geschichte des interreligiösen Dialogs, Berlin, 2019.

as a time characterised by a remarkable degree of tolerance between the monotheistic religions.[3]

A second aspect was the issue of truth and finding answers to basic questions of human life, which play a role in all religions. Traditions of faith connect people of the same or similar beliefs, world views, values and cultural expressions. In human history, an exchange across religious boundaries was partly based on the apology of one's own conviction and the demands of one's own superiority. There was also genuine curiosity, interest and openness to other cultures. Medieval theologians and philosophers such as Petrus Abaelard, Raimundus Lullus, and Nikolaus of Cues are examples of the first case, and Goethe's West-Eastern Divan is an example of an interest in cultural exchange.

To give another example, both aspects are blended in the concept of the »Confession of the unity of God« (tauhīd-i ilāhī) which was introduced by the Grand Mughal Akbar in Northern India in 1582.[4] After consultations with representatives of Islam, Hinduism and Buddhism he created this concept by establishing »Rules of universal peace« and adoring the sun as the universal religious basis and the symbol of light, God and the idea of the supreme good. He himself claimed to be the incarnation and the role model of this interreligious unity. But this sovereign measure that intended to integrate the different religious affiliations of the subjects of his realm has hardly survived his lifetime.

The idea of mutual tolerance played a central role in the Enlightenment movements in Europe at the end of the 18th century. The drama »Nathan the Wise« of Gotthold Ephraim Lessing and its Ring Parable mark an important turning point for the coexistence of religions. In the Ring Parable, no decision is made as to which religion is the true, the better or the convincing one. Rather, the question of truth loses its relevance to the goal of achieving mutual respect, tolerance and peaceful coexistence.

The Parliament of Religions of the World, held in Chicago in 1893, is seen as a very important historical milestone in terms of cooperation between world religions. Its goals were formulated in the invitation text to this event, which took place as part of a World Exhibition that was supposed to celebrate the »discovery« of America by Christopher Columbus 400

---

[3]   Dehn, op. cit., p. 23ff.
[4]   Ibid., p. 87ff.

years ago: »1. To bring together in conference, for the first time in history, the leading representatives of the great historic religions of the world. 2. To show to men, in the most impressive way, that and how many important truths the various religions hold and teach in common. 3. To promote and deepen the spirit of human brotherhood among religious men of various faith, through friendly conference and mutual good understanding, while not seeking to foster the temper of indifferentism, and not striving to achieve any formal and outward unity.«[5]

This event was an important and far-reaching step, as numerous other historical developments moved into a similar direction. Enlightenment thinking promoted freedom of thought and tolerance, which found political and social expression in democratic societies. In areas of Christian mission, especially in Africa and Asia, representatives of Western Christianity came into contact with other religions and also raised the question of the cooperation among the different churches. The Ecumenical movement developed as a worldwide Christian collaboration at the beginning of the 20th century. The establishment of international political cooperation and crisis management by the League of Nations and after the end of the Second World War, in 1945, the establishment of the United Nations as a recognised subject of international law took place, which, according to its charter, aims to promote international cooperation, to ensure world peace, to monitor the compliance with international law and to protect human rights.

In the second half of the 20th century, a large number of interreligious initiatives came into being, which cannot be listed here individually. Among them are those which strive for dialogue between two neighbouring religions or for closer cooperation between monotheistic religions. There are also initiatives that want to include as many religious communities as possible. Since some are active at regional, others at the national or international level, the field is very diverse. Among these, however, the vision of Hans Küng is worth mentioning, who stated in his programmatic study »Project Global Ethic« in 1990 the following three theses:

»No peace among nations without peace among religions. No peace between religions without dialogue between the religions. No dialogue between religions without basic research in religions.«[6]

---

[5] Quoted ibid., p. 115.
[6] Küng, Walter, Weltethos für Weltpolitik und Weltwirtschaft (World Ethos for World Pol-

In 1993, 200 representatives of world religions signed a corresponding declaration at the meeting of the »Parliament of World Religions«, which included the »Golden Rule« of reciprocity, the commitment to non-violence, justice and truthfulness and the partnership between women and men. Since the historical initiatives mentioned were both responses to and shaped by contemporary challenges, it is no coincidence that Religions for Peace was founded in a time when the nuclear arms race threatened humanity and advancing globalisation posed – in addition to many possibilities and amenities – new forms of threats and conflicts and made the question of shared global responsibility inevitable.

Against this background, the focus and goals of interreligious cooperation at the global level will be presented and analysed in this article using Religions for Peace International as an example. In the first chapter I will take a look at the development of this organisation since its foundation and the challenges and topics that have been addressed. The second chapter focuses on the Strategic Plan 2020–2025 to present some current priorities and goals of this international movement. In a third part, this Plan will be analysed in the light of the development of Religions for Peace over the past decades in order to elaborate the profile of the network. In the last section, a summary outlook aims to classify and evaluate this work.

1. »Cooperating effectively for Peace« – mission and vision of Religions for Peace

Religions for Peace was founded in 1970, but its origins date back to 1961 when some senior representatives of the world's major faith traditions started to explore possibilities to convene religious summits and to take common action toward peace.[7] Today, the global Religions for Peace network is »comprised of the World Council with its International Secretariat; 6 regional and 90 national inter-religious councils; the Global Women of

---

itics and World Economy), München/Zürich 1997, p. 131.
[7] See also the chapter on the historical background, the foundation and the history of Religions for Peace in: Dehn, op. cit., p. 135ff.

Faith Network; Global Interfaith Youth Network; and their religious constituencies«.[8]

The Religions for Peace movement understands itself as »*guided by the vision of a world in which religious communities cooperate effectively for Peace, by taking concrete common action*«[9]. This vision is presently translated into a mission statement as follows:

> »Multi-religious cooperation for Peace as shared well-being is the hallmark of RfP. This cooperation includes but also goes beyond dialogue and bears fruit in common concrete action. Through RfP, diverse religious communities discern ›deeply held and widely shared‹ moral concerns, such as violent conflict; gender inequality; environmental degradation; threats to the freedom of thought, conscience and religion; lack of inter-religious understanding; and the shrinking space for civil society and multilateralism. RfP translates theses shared concerns into concrete multi-religious action.«[10]

According to its organisational structure Religions for Peace is active at the community, national, regional and global level.

In order to get an idea of the work of this international network the following short summary of the World Assemblies, their topics and final declarations can offer some information and insights.

The first World Assembly of Religions for Peace[11] was convened in Kyoto, Japan, in October 1970 under the theme »Advancing Peace through Disarmament, Development and Human Rights«. The final declaration reports that this meeting brought together »man and women of all major religions«, namely from Bahai, Buddhist, Confucian, Christian, Hindi, Jain, Jewish, Muslim, Shintoist, Sikh, Zoroastrian and others traditions[12]. Some main principles were stated: The common conviction that we »*are now united in one destiny. We live or die together in the struggle for peace*«[13]. Peace is explained by the three topics: disarmament, development and human rights. The corresponding necessary action are formulated as follows: »*We must do all to educate public opinion and awaken public conscience to*

---

8   www.rfp.org.
9   Religions for Peace, Strategic Plan 2020–2025, New York 2020, p. 5.
10   Ibid., p. 5.
11   The initial name »World Conference on Religions for Peace« was later changed into »Religions for Peace«.
12   The Kyoto Declaration of the First World Assembly, Kyoto 1970, p. 1; this final declaration and those of the following World Assemblies can be accessed online at www.rfp.org/about/world-assemblies/.
13   Ibid., p. 2.

take a firm stand against war.«[14] A strong cooperation was identified as needed not only among religions but also with those outside the historic religions. The partnership with the United Nations was foreseen to take a leadership role in main parts of world politics.

The following 1974 World Assembly was held in Leuven, Belgium, under the title »World Religions, World Peace«. Beside the notion of peace the term »liberation« was a key word of the conference. In 1979, the third Assembly in Princeton, USA, chose the headline »Religion in the Struggle for World Community« and was attended by 354 delegates from 47 countries representing the mentioned religious traditions. The mobilisation for peace was explained in five sections: through struggle for a just international economic order, for nuclear and conventional disarmament, for human rights, in response to the environment and energy crisis and by promoting education for peace. The fourth World Assembly in 1984 took place in Nairobi, Kenya. 600 delegates from 60 countries dealt with the theme: »Religions for Human Dignity and World Peace«. As the assembly was held in Africa, traditional cultures of Africa and North America came into the spotlight as well as 150 women leaders from interfaith cooperation networks and beyond as well es over 100 youth delegates representing the »vitality and vision of a new generation«[15].

The World Assembly in 1989 took place in a nuclear weapon-free zone in Melbourne, Australia, under the headline »Building Peace Through Trust«. Nearly 600 delegates from 60 countries attended, among them thirty-five percent of women and fifteen percent young delegates. A women's meeting and a youth conference preceded the main conference. The assembly was aware of the political changes following the end of the Cold War and, in looking forward to the new millennium, expressed signs of hope like »*an increased awareness of the importance of moral values in human life*«[16]. Peace building was illustrated by promoting trust.

With nearly 1,000 participants, the next conference in 1994 in Rome (Vatican) and Riva del Garda, Italy, was significantly bigger and again included also gatherings of women and youth delegates. The topic »Healing the World: Religions for Peace« was the focal point to discuss elements of

---

[14] Ibid., p. 2.
[15] The Nairobi Declaration of the 4th World Assembly, Nairobi 1984, p. 1.
[16] The Melbourne Declaration of the 5th World Assembly, Melbourne 1998, p. 2.

peace building including the situation of children worldwide. In 1999, the World Assembly took place in Amman, Jordan, with the theme »Action for Common Living«. Delegates from 70 countries and 15 religious traditions were aware of the symbolic marking of time just at the eve of the third millennium and placed the idea of »common humanity« into the centre of the gathering.

Held again in Kyoto, Japan, the eighth World Assembly in 2006 dealt with »Confronting Violence and Advancing Shared Security«. The emphasis was on facing and overcoming violence through a multi-faith response and by fostering shared security. In 2013, the gathering was convened in Vienna, Austria, under the headline »Welcoming the Other – Advancing Human Dignity, Citizenship and Shared Well-Being«. Over 600 delegates from 90 national councils and groups including indigenous participants and delegates of the women's and youth's networks attended the meeting. The rising hostility against migrants, refugees and people of other cultural and religious backgrounds was the reason behind a multireligious vision of peace through »welcoming the other«.

Besides this overview on the history of Religions for Peace, a closer look should be taken at the consultations at the tenth World Assembly as they provides the substructure of the Strategic Plan 2020–2025 and the platform for present strategies and activities of Religions for Peace worldwide.

This gathering took place in 2019 on the island of Lindau, Germany, dealing with »Caring for our Common Future – Advancing Shared Well-Being«. Approximately 1,000 delegates from 125 countries attended the gathering. Five commissions of Religions for Peace International presented results of their preparatory work to the Assembly which were summarised in commission reports[17]. These reports are linked to the five sub-themes of the meeting:

1) Advancing Shared Well-Being as a Multi-religious Vision of Positive Peace[18]
2) Advancing Shared Well-Being by Preventing and Transforming Violent Conflicts[19]

---

[17] See Workbook of the 10th World Assembly, Lindau/Germany 2019.
[18] Workbook, p. 3–25.
[19] Workbook, p. 24–54.

3) Advancing Shared Well-Being by Promoting Just and Harmonious Societies[20]

4) Advancing Shared Well-Being by Promoting Integral Human Development[21]

5) Advancing Shared Well-Being by Protecting the Earth[22]

The consultation process during the Assembly resulted in the adoption of a final declaration[23]. This document comprises not only the main findings of the topics of the conference but also Action Points which, among other proposals, take up and support already existing declarations and campaigns like the »Charter for Forgiveness and Reconciliation«, the »International Campaign to Abolish Nuclear Weapons«, the »Faiths for Forest Declaration« and the »Interfaith Rainforest Initiative«.[24]

The final declaration can be summarised concerning actions points as follows:

Topic	Action Points
Multi-Religious Vision of Positive Peace (corresponding to Commission 1)	Charter for Forgiveness and Reconciliation
Preventing and Transforming Violent Conflicts (corresponding to Commission 2)	International Campaign to Abolish Nuclear Weapons
Promoting Just and Harmonious Societies (corresponding to Commission 3)	Alliance of Virtue
Promoting Integral Human Development / Protecting the Earth (corresponding to Commissions 4 and 5)	Faith for Forest Declaration Interfaith Rainforest Initiative Sustainable Development Goals

---

[20] Workbook, p. 55–86.
[21] Workbook, p. 87–105.
[22] Workbook, p. 107–146.
[23] See www.rfp.org.
[24] Background information and details to the Action Points are complied in the brochure »Action Points for the Commissions of the Religions for Peace 10th World Assembly«, New York 2020.

Religions for Peace did not only want to formulate a declaration and public statements but also to translate and implement the commitments into concrete action. Therefore, the transfer of statements into actions are essential. The Religions for Peace Strategic Plans provide the implementation of goals for the period between two World Assemblies.

2. The Strategic Plan 2020–2025

2.1 Participatory preparation

The Strategic Plan 2020–2025 is the result of a planning process which is considered as the most inclusive and participatory one in the history of Religions for Peace.[25] The first and main basis was built by the mentioned preparation and consultations of the 10th World Assembly in Lindau and its final declaration.

In order to offer involvement and participation as broad as possible for developing the Strategic Plan, a questionnaire was sent out to participants and network partners worldwide asking to identify (1) the three top challenges/issues which can best be served by the multi-religious convening strength of Religions for Peace, (2) the three key opportunities to overcome these challenges through multi-religious action and (3) the sort of commitment to action, service and engagement the survey respondents could offer[26]. The results of this survey have been presented to the plenary of a global gathering in December 2019 in New York including around 250 representatives and stakeholders from all regions of the Religions for Peace network, religious traditions plus government officials, diplomats, United Nations representatives and leaders of partner organizations of Religions for Peace.[27]

The result of the survey[28] comprised of around 120 single items, was split up into six topics, i.e. (1) Peace and Security Considerations (positive and negative peace), (2) Environment, (3) Gender Justice, (4) Freedom of

---

[25] Strategic Plan, p. 1.
[26] See Call for Your Contribution to Religions for Peace Strategic Plan (2020–2025), New York 7 October 2019.
[27] See Religions for Peace, Multi-Religious & Multi-stakeholder Partnership for Peace & Development, 11–13 December 2019, New York (Conference invitation and documents)
[28] See Strategic Plan 2020–2025 – Summary of Survey Responses, New York 2019.

Thought, (5) Interreligious Education and (6) Interreligious Collaboration and Partnership and grouped into the clusters of »Challenges«, »Opportunities« and »Commitment to Action«. Compared to the main topics of the final document of the World Assembly the number of responses in the fields of education, training and awareness raising on the one hand and »cross cutting issues« on the other hand were remarkable and motivated to provide extra space for these aspects. The evaluation of the responses was enriched by further tables which linked the topics to the United Nations Sustainable Development Goals[29] and potential Sustainable Development Goals indicators for success[30].

2.2 Main elements of the Strategic Plan

The Strategic Plan takes as a starting point an analyses of »Our World Today« referring to a good number of global reports by different international research organisation and the United Nations[31]. In this setting of urgent global issues, the religious communities are challenged. There is a need for stronger cooperation between the faith-based organisations as it falls into their moral mandate to alleviate and overcome the current challenges. The United Nations have realised that religious communities should play an increasingly important role in this scenario hoping »*to benefit from the social capital available for sustainable human development, human rights, and peace and security*«[32].

The paragraph on »Vision, Mission and Principles« underlines that the cooperation the Religions for Peace movement offers »goes beyond dialogue and bears fruit in common concrete action«[33]. These activities are guided by seven principles: (1) respect religious differences; (2) leverage the existing spiritual, moral and social assets of the world's religious communities; (3) built and strengthen representative, sustainable inter-religious mechanisms, co-owned by religious communities; (4) act on deeply held

---

[29] Ibid., p. 2.
[30] Ibid., p. 12.
[31] Among others the UNHCR, the Institute for Economics and Peace, the World Economic Forum, Pew Research Center; see Strategic Plan (2020), p. 4.
[32] United Nations Population Fund (UNFPA), Religion and Development Post 2015. Report of a consultation among donor organisations, United Nations development agencies and faith-based organisations, New York 2014, p. xi; quoted in: Strategic Plan, p. 4.
[33] Ibid., p. 5.

and widely shared values; (5) honour the identity and community of each religious tradition; (6) link local, national, regional and global multi-religious structures and (7) forge partnership with other sectors of society.[34]

The strengths of Religions for Peace are seen in four aspects in addition to the common concern for the well-being of all and the combat against the abuse of religion.[35] First, multi-religious cooperation can be more powerful and stop conflicts. Second, the inter-religious structures – including the Global Women of Faith Network and the Interfaith Youth Network – are self-led and can build bridges between different religious communities. Third, the main agents for common actions are the religious communities themselves. Religions for Peace can assist to analyse specific problems, to make an inventory of the strengths of the respective communities and identify areas of capacity building. Fourthly, Religions for Peace has amassed through its 50 years history a great amount of experience in different fields of common action which offers a solid basis for further plans.

The Strategic Plan describes six strategic goals which mainly mirrors the above mentioned topics of the World Assembly's outcomes and the responses of the survey – albeit in a different order and composition. The individual points can only be summarised in the following selection.

1) The first Strategic goal »Promote Peaceful, Just and Inclusive Societies« encompasses a number of different activities which also support several Sustainable Development Goals (SDGs) of the United Nations[36]. Therefore, the partnership with different branches of the United Nations is recommended. The transformation of conflicts needs further commitment including the objectives of the agenda for forgiveness and reconciliation explained in the Charter for Forgiveness and Reconciliation[37]. The first goal includes also public health challenges, measures for good

---

[34] Ibid., p. 5; the wording of those principles varies in different documents (see also five principles on www.rfp.org).

[35] Ibid., p. 6–9.

[36] The Sustainable Development Goals (SDGs) are 17 political goals of the United Nations (UN), which should serve to ensure sustainable development on an economic, social and ecological level worldwide. They came into effect in 2016 with a term of 15 years, i.e. until 2030; therefore the Sustainable Development Goals are also called »Agenda 2030«. These Goals affects all countries, in contrast to the Millennium Development Goals (MDGs), which particularly applied to developing countries.

[37] also available on www.charterforforgiveness.org.

government and implementation of international law, a general disarmament, poverty alleviation strategies, peace building by mediation and the negotiation and care for migrants and refugees.

2) »Advance Gender Equality« is the headline of Strategic goal 2. This goal underlines in particular the promotion of women's leadership by dissemination and implementation of women's rights and promotion of women led initiatives. The link to respective topics of the Sustainable Development Goals are again stressed. Last but not least, safe space should be created for dialogue on lesbian, gay, bisexual and transgender issues (LGBT) and concepts of sex education.

3) The Strategic goal 3 is »Nurture a Sustainable Environment« and emphasises that religious communities have always cared for all forms of life. With this strategic goal Religions for Peace intends to protect and restore the endangered ecosystem of our planet. Raising of awareness should be aimed achieving a change of lifestyle including the Interfaith Rainforest Initiative and the cooperation with indigenous communities and their elders. Educating and lobbying politicians and policy makers can be linked with data analysis to combat environmental degradation.

4) The topic of Strategic goal 4 is »Champion Freedom of Thought, Conscience and Religion«. This objective intents to enforce the human right enshrined in Article 18 of the Universal Declaration of Human Rights to »advance a more robust notion of citizenship«[38]. Awareness building and providing safe space for reflection and political actions are focal points in this field of concern. A number of declarations and campaigns are listed: The Alliance of Virtue which is one Action Point of the 10th World Assembly of Religions for Peace in Lindau, the United Nations Plan of Action to Safeguard Religious Sites[39], the United Nations Strategy and Plan of Action in Hate Speech[40], the Marrakesh Declaration[41] and the Beirut Declaration and Commitment on Faith of Rights[42].

---

[38] Strategic Plan, p. 14.
[39] See United Nations Alliance of Civilisations, In Unity and Solidarity for Safe and Peaceful Worship, 2019. At the World Assembly in Lindau a »Ring of Peace«, a big wooden art construction, was erected in the centre of the location to establish a symbol against all sorts of menace and threats to places of worship and to reaffirm the legal protection of holy places.
[40] See United Nations Office on Genocide Prevention and the Responsibility to Protect, United Nations Strategy Plan of Action on Hate Speech, New York 2019.

5) Strategic goal 5 aims to »Strengthen inter-religious Education«. Inter-religious education should be promoted »to increase trust and improve understanding, respect and relationship between people of different faith«[43]. This includes activities to foster religious literacy by lessons and interfaith training programs and exchange preferably among children and young people. It should also include research and concept development as well as organisation of interfaith celebrations and festivals like the World Interfaith Harmony Week[44] and the International Day of Tolerance[45].

6) »Foster Multi-religious Collaboration and Global Partnership Strategic« is the objective of Strategic goal 6. In order to strengthen the capacity for collaboration, the partnership between religious communities and interfaith groups on each level should be scaled up as well as the cooperation with governmental and intergovernmental entities and other partners active in different fields of concern. The media and partners who can disseminate success stories are important as well as contact to organisations helping to raise resources.

Four key methods of operationalisation are recommended to implement these goals[46]. First, advocacy means to influence public debates and thoughts, to raise awareness and influence specific actors. Secondly, capacity building should be implemented by training for actors of religions communities and by offering safe space for dialogue and action. Thirdly, knowledge management can be enhanced by disseminating statements and declarations to equip in particular people in leading positions with shared convictions and strategies. Fourth, humanitarian support can be provided by humanitarian relief, spiritual support, medical treatment and inter-religions prayers and assistance.

---

[41] See Marrakesh Declaration on the Right of Religious Minorities in Predominantly Muslim Majority Communities, 2016 (www.marrakeshdeclaration.org).

[42] See Office of the United Nations High Commissioner for Human Rights, The Beirut Declaration and its 18 commitments on Faith for Rights, Geneva 2019 (www.ohchr.org/Documents).

[43] Strategic Plan, p. 14.

[44] The World Interfaith Harmony Week was proposed by H.M. King Abdullah II of Jordan to the United Nations. In 2010, the United Nations General Assembly unanimously adopted this proposal recommending to celebrate this Week in the first week of February.

[45] In 1996, the United Nations General Assembly invited the member states to observe 16 November as International Day for Tolerance.

[46] Strategic Plan, p. 10f.

The last chapter of the Strategic Plan under the title »Monitoring Progress, Measuring Outcomes«[47] contains a list of all mentioned activities of the six strategic goals. 34 items are summarised in terms of indicators, the expected output or outcome and the link to respective Sustainable Development Goals. Throughout this table, the indicators are the expected number of the respective activities and the expected output or outcome will be measured by an increase of awareness or an improvement in the appropriate field of activities.

The Strategic Plan does not contain any indication who will implement the single action points and what sort and what amount of personal and financial resources are available to put these very ambitious agendas into practice. As it is mentioned that the strategic priorities adopted by the World Council do not preclude activities by members within the other areas of the movement and that each member is free to set own priorities, an indication is missing who will be in charge of the implementation of the individual measures.

3. Religions as civil actors – the current profile of global strategies

After the quick glance at the previous tradition and the current strategy of Religions for Peace, some aspects will now be analysed in more detail. How does the strategic plan reveal a profile of interreligious cooperation and how does this fit into the work of Religions for Peace so far?

3.1 Different faiths – common action

The name »Religions for peace« contains quite clearly and in a nutshell the program of the movement: People from different religious traditions feel united in a common goal, namely the commitment to peace. The wording »Different faiths – common action«[48] expresses very precisely that there is a basic view despite religious and cultural differences. The re-

---

[47]   Ibid., p. 18–23.
[48]   Religions for Peace International presents its expanded and revised website at www.rfp.org under the headline »Different Faiths – Common Action«.

lationship of the two elements are clearly expressed in the Declaration of Nairobi: We are »*rooted in our religious traditions, and linked to one another in vision and action*«[49].

The term »peace« is the focal point of the joint engagement. This notion is a very broad term with a utopian vision.[50] It includes both religious and philosophical as well as political and practical dimensions. With regard to the religious anchoring of the term in the various traditions it is explained that each religion knows and anticipates peace to be a »positive« holistic state of personal and social flourishing that is far more than the absence of conflict. Words like »shalom, salaam and shanti are cyphers for these holistic and positive religious visions«[51]. The Leuven Declaration of 1974 states: »Peace is a supreme value for all religions.«[52] The practical and political dimension of the term is expressed in the Princeton Declaration, 1979, with the following wording: »*World community, built in love, freedom, justice and truth, is another name for peace.*«[53]

It has been apparent since the movement was founded that there has been no attempt anywhere to formulate a common religious belief or creed. In the »Executive Summary« of the Strategic Plan, the following is explained regarding the common ground:

»For RfP, Peace has always been more than the absence of war or violence. The advancement of human dignity and shared well-being in harmony with the earth is at the heart of RfP's positive vision of Peace, a multi-religious vision expressed in terms of shared values, not doctrines.«[54]

By outspokenly denying »doctrines«, Religions for Peace does not interpret religious or theological teaching as a starting point for its basis. Differences in teaching are deliberately left as they are. Nevertheless, common convictions as basis for joint action must of course be clarified.

Taking into account the diversity of religious traditions and beliefs, the underlying religious beliefs are left with a certain vagueness. The terms

---

[49] The Nairobi Declaration of the 4th World Assembly, Nairobi 1984, p. 1.
[50] Concerning the role of fuzzy terms see: Affolderbach, Martin / Scheunpflug, Annette, Zur Funktion unscharfer Begriffe. Ein Plädoyer für einen reflexiven Blick auf Explikationen (On the function of fuzzy terms. A plea for a reflexive look at explications), in: Vierteljahrsschrift für wissenschaftliche Pädagogik 95 (2019) Paderborn, p. 187–198.
[51] Www.rfp.org.
[52] The Leuven Declaration of the 2nd World Assembly, Leuven, 1974, p. 2.
[53] The Princeton Declaration of the 3th World Assembly, Princeton, 1979, p. 1.
[54] Strategic Plan, p. 2.

and formulations change. Sometimes one speaks of the »Saint« or of »God or the truth in which we believe«[55] or of the »higher spiritual power«[56] or the »horizon of the Ultimate«[57]. The fact of religious diversity is described as »perceived as God given, a reflection of a divine nature, derived from cosmic laws, inherent sacredness or oneness with the universe«[58].

With this in mind, it is understandable that religious prayers, services or rituals are included with particular caution. In the Princeton Declaration the final sentence contains a relatively vague request: »*We shall pray or mediate, as well as work, that this new ear may be realized.*«[59] The final paragraph of the Melbourne Declaration sounds somehow like a prayer as all five sentences starts with the words »Lead us from fear to trust. Lead us ...« leaving open to whom this sort of prayer is directed.[60] Only the Nairobi Declaration mentioned religious services explicitly: »We have shared in worship and meditation.«[61] Common religious ceremonies, prayers or services are the exception like an Indian ceremony addressing four directions of the winds which was celebrated in the plenary of the Lindau Assembly in the context of the section on »Protecting the Earth«.

However, the question remains how the commonalities of the collaboration are formulated. This will be analysed in the next section.

3.2 Shared values

The recognition of the diversity of religions constitutes the undisputed backbone of collaboration. In fact, there never have been critical questions or comments towards single religious convictions. A »common concern for peace« is the starting point for building a joint coalition. The diagnosis of a crisis or a current challenge leads to joint actions.

This is stated in the declaration of the founding assembly in Kyoto as follows:

---

[55] Princeton, p. 2.
[56] Melbourne, p. 2.
[57] The Riva del Garda Declaration of the 6th World Assembly, Riva del Garda 1994, p. 2; The »horizon of the Ultimate« is interpreted as »healing and harmony«.
[58] The Amman Declaration of the 7th World Assembly, Amman 1999, p. 1.
[59] Princeton, p. 4.
[60] Melbourne, p. 4f.
[61] Nairobi, p. 2.

»We have come together in peace out of a common concern for peace... We found that we share:
A conviction of the fundamental unity of the human family, and the equality and dignity of all human beings;
A sense of the sacredness of the individual person and his conscience;
A sense of the value of the human community;
A realization that might is not right; that human power is not self-sufficien and absolute;
A belief that love, compassion, selflessness, and the force of inner truthfulness and of the spirit have ultimately greater power than hate, enmity, and self-interest;
A sense of obligation to stand on the side of the poor and the oppressed as against the rich and the oppressors; and
A profound hope that good will finally prevail.
Because of these convictions that we hold in common, we believe thata special charge has been given to all men and women of religion to be concerned with all their hearts and minds with peace and peacemaking, to be the servants of peace.«[62]

In the declaration of the third World Assembly in Princeton, this is worded as follows:

»Adhering to different religions, we may differ in our objects of faith and worship. Nevertheless, in the way we practice our faith, we all confess that the God or the truth in which we believe transcends the powers and divisions of this world. We are not masters, but servants and witnesses, always being changed and disciplined in worship, meditation, and practice by the truth which we confess. We all acknowledge restraint and self-discipline in a community of giving and forgiving love as basic to human life and the form of true blessedness.

We are all commanded by our faiths to seek justice in the world in community of free and equal persons. In this search, conscience is given to every person as a moral guide to the ways of truth among us all. We believe that peace in world community is not only possible but is the way of life for human beings on earth, as we learn it in our prayers or meditation and by our faiths. These convictions we share. Therefore we can go further and share a common confidence about the fruits of religious witness in the world.«[63]

As these two quotes already show, the respective terms in the declarations of the World Assemblies are quite different. The »multi-faith identity« relates to a »multi-religious vision of positive peace«[64]. The Melbourne declaration speaks of »common commitment«[65], elsewhere of »common humanity« and »conscience« as a »moral guide«[66]. The term »shared values«

---

[62]   Kyoto 1970, p. 1.
[63]   Princeton, p. 3.
[64]   Strategic Plan, p. 6.
[65]   Melbourne, p. 1.
[66]   Princeton, p. 2: »Conscience is given to every person as a moral guide.«

is used in the current documents. The Strategic Plan states that the strategic goals of Religions for Peace are »*based upon deeply held moral principles widely shared by the world's faith traditions*«[67]. These »shared values« can be found both in the formulations that define peace as a common goal and in the »guiding principles« that are cited above[68] in the formulation of the Strategic Plan. Elsewhere, the Strategic Plan speaks of the »moral mandate of the world's religious communities«[69].

The slightly different wording and the changing terms of these ethical principles as well as the evolving adjustment of the principles show clearly that this development is the result of a comprehensive current discourse. The Strategic Plan explicitly speaks of »five decades of learning«, which the movement can look back on.[70]

We will see below that at this point there is a strong cross-connection to the global discourse on human rights and guiding political principles. This connection is repeatedly made in the statements of Religions for Peace. In the documents for the World Assembly in Lindau, this basis is referred to as a »modern order«[71] and it is added rightly and with concern that this basis is being questioned in some current political developments.[72] »Modern order« appears in these documents as the »à qui«, which means the entirety of what has been achieved in such clarification processes so far.

Obviously, a better clarification of these foundations is sought, as the Strategic Plan contains in its catalogue of tasks a reference to the Charter of the New Alliance of Virtues[73]. This document seeks a well-argued reli-

---

[67] Strategic Plan, p. 11f.
[68] P. 98f.
[69] Strategic Plan, p. 4.
[70] Ibid., p. 2.
[71] Workbook, p. 5ff.
[72] In the Workbook, p. 10f, three »enemies« of community are named: (1) ignorance, (2) individual egoism and (3) group egoism.
[73] Strategic Goal 4, Action Point 3. The Charter of the New Alliance of Virtues (www.al-lianceofvirtues.com) which was mainly drafted by the Forum for Promoting Peace in Muslim Societies and its president Shaykh Abdullah bin Bayyah, who currently also serves as a co-moderator of Religions for Peace International, is focused on the »rights that exist prior to the state and inhere in each human being by virtue of his or her existence. Such rights are typically understood as deriving from a greater-than-human source, such as God or nature, for the believer or non-believer. These rights must be acknowledged and protected by any just state. They should be understood as necessary to human dignity, as well as social flourishing.« The »shared values« are explained in nine principles: Human Dignity, freedom of conscience and religion or belief, tolerance, justice, peace, mercy, kindness, keeping covenants and solidarity. (Art 4)

gious foundation of shared values and virtues. Starting from religious similarities between the Abrahamic religions, the elaboration of the »virtues« should be seen in congruence to international conventions and human rights declarations.

Beside this, the United Nations Sustainable Development Goals play obviously an important role in regard to the practical implementation of common goals. In the Strategic Plan, these goals are a very important point of reference in terms of global recognition of strategic objectives and their implementation. One aspect might be that Religions for Peace expects to profit from certain budget lines of the United Nations to implement some of their actions points.

3.3 The ambivalence of religions

In the history of mankind, religions have not always been agents and actors of peace and tolerance, but also too often the source of demarcation, hostility and justification for war and cruelty. Even today, tolerance and peaceful cooperation between religions are by no means a matter of course everywhere.

The founding members of Religions for Peace were obviously very aware of this challenge when they formulated 1970 in the Kyoto Declaration:

»As men and women of religion we confess in humility and penitence that we have very often betrayed our religious ideals and our commitment to peace. It is not religion that has failed the cause of peace, but religious people. This betrayal of religion can and must be corrected.«[74]

Such formulations are regularly found in the declarations of the World Assemblies. It is acknowledged that religions have been used too often to justify warfare and community strife or have not raised their voices against violations of ethical principles.[75] Religious fanaticism, religious nationalism and extremism are denounced and religion is identified as a cause of divisions[76]. The Lindau Declaration states: »*Our hearts grieve over the misuse of*

---

[74] Kyoto 1970, p. 1.
[75] Princeton, p. 1; Nairobi, p. 1f; The Kyoto Declaration of the 8th World Assembly, Kyoto 2006, p. 1.
[76] Melbourne, p. 2; Riva del Garda, p. 2.

our faiths, especially the ways they have been twisted to fuel violence and hate.«[77]
The Kyoto Assembly of 2006 addresses its own constituency when saying:
»*Religious communities and leaders must stand up, speak out, and take action
against the misuse of religion.*«[78]

As counterpart to the terms »misuse« and »abuse« of religion[79] the notion of »authentic religion« is set.[80] It is beyond the merit of this publication
to discus in detail whether it is correct and appropriate to distinguish between a specific religion as the realm of peaceful beliefs on the one hand
and on the other hand its followers – or maybe (minority) groups of the
followers – who misused this belief. It can hardly be denied that the foundations of numerous religions themselves contain both: the search for salvation and redemption as well as the messages of peace and well-being on
the one side and on the other side explicit or implicit statements and convictions that can fuel disassociation, demarcation, confrontation to »non-
believers« and hate. Such passages, for example in holy scriptures, are in
fact still used by religious groups to justify selfish, aggressive, inhuman
behaviour or terrorist acts.

With regard to obvious extremism and fanaticism, it is undoubtedly
justified to speak of an »abuse« of religion and to take appropriate demar-
cations and measures. However, it is more difficult to assess the fact that
religious communities and their leaders do not always share the goals described by Religions for Peace as »authentic religion«. Although religions
have renewed and reformed themselves over the course of their history
and have also responded to criticism and taken on new challenges such as
those caused by a new world view and the technical revolutions of modern
times, there are also numerous groups and movements in the field of religions that have a traditional world view and maintain, defend and proclaim
very conservative beliefs. In addition, it is not uncommon for religions to
be associated with cultural hegemony and political claims to power. This
danger is particularly great where state power is combined with a certain
religious belief or where religious leaders attract state power.

---

[77] The Lindau Declaration of the 10th World Assembly, Lindau 2019, Preamble.
[78] Kyoto 2006, p. 2.
[79] See for example Kyoto 2006, p. 2, 4 and 5; The Vienna Declaration of the 9th World As-
      sembly, Vienna 2013, p. 1; Lindau, p. 1 and Strategic Plan, p. 2.
[80] Riva del Garda, p. 2.

The goal of striving for peace, justice and human rights is therefore not only a requirement aimed at members of a society, the public and those responsible for politics, but also to their own religious fellows. It is therefore consistent and appropriate that appeals made by Religions for Peace are primarily directed at the religious communities[81]. In the final section of the »Multi-religious Call to Action« of the 2006 Kyoto Declaration, seven points which refer to changes in one's own religious communities are mentioned in the first position.[82]

Given the sometimes ambivalent role of religious communities or religious groups, it is understandable that state and international organisations take a certain neural or critical distance from some of them, as they sometimes represent particular interests. A common good orientation is not always shared as a matter of course. The above-mentioned agreement between the United Nations and religious communities[83] is an expression of the fact that such a relationship is possible, but was and is in no way always taken for granted. The activities and confidence-building measures of Religions for Peace vis-à-vis the United Nations, governments and other political partners must be regarded particularly positively.

3.4 Thematic development

The topic »peace« was the starting point at the inception of Religions for Peace. In a certain sense this focus reflects also the general political climate at this period of time. In this section I will respond to the question of whether this topic has remained and further developed or whether there have been changes in the thematic program. If so, what were the reasons for these changes? Was it caused by a deeper understanding of the topic or was it due to the political framework and the associated global challenges?

---

[81] Already the declaration of the First World Assembly in Kyoto finished with appeals to different target groups, in the first place: »We speak to our religions, the ecumenical councils and all interfaith efforts for peace...« (p. 1).

[82] Kyoto 2006, p. 5. The seven items are in brief: resisting any misuse of religion, becoming effective educators for conflict transformation, educating members to advance shared security, strengthening peace education, holding governments accountable, fostering multi-religious cooperation and partnership with governments and other organisations for shared security.

[83] See above footnote 32.

At the first World Assembly, the general context was the fear of nuclear weapons. So, the issue of disarmament and resistance to a progressive nuclear rearmament was the main focus of the consultations. References to the issue of global development have been seen against the background that such armament was taking away resources from poverty alleviation.

In 1974 this connection was clearly underlined in Leuven by the description of the human destiny as the starting point of the consultations. The concept of freedom formed a second centring point. Freedom of belief is one of the human rights worth to be mentioned in this context. The spiritual perspective also played a special role in this meeting.

»As each of us turns to prayer and meditation, we seek a conversion of heart to bring about the spirit of sacrifice, humility, and self-restraint which will further justice, development, liberation, and peace.«[84]

The respect of people vis-à-vis to the nature and the »mystery of existence« must lead to the »value of humble self-restraint«[85].

The third World Assembly in 1979 in Princeton considered itself at »*a turning point in human history, with the survival of world civilization at stake*«[86] and developed five subtopics for »our work for peace, justice, and human dignity«[87], namely (1) a just international economic order, (2) nuclear and conventional disarmament, (3) human rights, (4) environment and energy crisis and (5) education for peace. The political demands on arms limitation (referencing to SALT I and II negotiations) and on a more leading role of the United Nations were made explicit.

In Nairobi, the participants complained about »too little progress« and advocated »time for new strategies and priorities for peacemaking«[88]. In addition to the special focus on the situation in Africa and the first-time admission of migrants and refugees as a relevant problem, the focus of the meeting was on (1) reconciliation in regional conflicts, (2) disarmament, (3) development, (4) human rights and (5) peace education.

The Melbourne declaration explained a number of signs of hope, among them also »an increased awareness of the importance of moral values in

---

[84]   Leuven, p. 4.
[85]   Ibid., p. 3.
[86]   Princeton, p. 1.
[87]   Princeton, p. 1.
[88]   Nairobi, p. 1.

human life«[89]. »Building Peace Through Trust« was the recommended strategy of promoting peace[90].

The 6th World Assembly took place at a »time of transition, as the world passes from the Cold War to a new order yet uncertain«[91]. Religions should seek a third way in alternative to capitalism and Marxism. In compliance with the topic of the meeting »Healing the World: Religions for Peace«, peace was translated into processes of healing. The dramatic situation of 18.5 million refugees and 20 million displaced people was taken up and special attention was paid to the situation of children and the endangered earth.

The topic »Action for Common Living« of the Amman World Assembly in 1999 is explained by fostering a culture of peace in underlining common humanity, common security, common interdependence and common future. The development of non-violent methodologies of conflict resolution must go parallel with the calls for disarmament and the elimination of (nuclear) weapons. Transmitting the values of peace and just and sustainable development into the third Millennium is a main task for peace education.

The 2006 World Assembly in Kyoto explained the theme »Confronting Violence and Advancing Shared Security« by the insight that, in particular, the misuse of religions should be challenged by multi-religious cooperation. The final declaration addressed, for the first time, specific groups by calling them for action: (1) the religious communities themselves, (2) the global network of Religions for Peace and (3) the governments, the international organisations and the business sector. All people of good will are invited to collaborate with religious communities, too.[92] This particular address to target groups was repeated in the declaration of the Assembly in 2013 in Vienna which dealt with the topic »Welcoming the Other – A Multi-Religious Vision of Peace« as the rising hostility in many regions required a strongly proclaimed culture of hospitality.

The five sub themes of the Lindau Assembly »Advancing Shared Well-Being as a Multi-religious Vision of Positive Peace, by Preventing and Transforming Violent Conflicts, by Promoting Just and Harmonious Soci-

---

[89] Melbourne, p. 2.
[90] Ibid., p. 3.
[91] Riva del Garda, p. 1.
[92] Kyoto 2006, p. 4f.

eties, by Promoting Integral Human Development and by Protecting the Earth« were well in line with the main previous topics. The current concern was the observation that there is a »meta-crisis« questioning the values and objectives of a discourse on a global level accompanied by (national) selfishness and intended fake news. The declaration strived for greater commitment among the participants in order to compel them to implementing the numerous action points. In Lindau, a separate focus was laid on conflict management as a number of religious leaders from countries of conflict convened privately for peace talks. The symbol of a Ring of Peace[93] was erected to call for a protection of places of worship worldwide, an initiative mentioned for the first time in the Vienna Assembly 2013[94].

In summary, the following threads can be identified in this discourse tradition spanning over five decades. The three main themes of 1970, namely »peace, development and human rights« have persisted and have been deepened and expanded upon in various dimensions.

- *Peace:* The special accent on disarmament runs through from 1970 to Lindau 2019. New aspects have been added primarily focussing on the social dimension of peace, namely the role of social peace, different forms of violence, the culture of welcoming the other and, in particular, conflict management, mediation, reconciliation and peace talks aiming at the settlement of conflicts.
- *Development:* The starting point was the commitment to structures of a just economic order. The African perspective in Nairobi broadened, in particular, the view on sharing resources not only as a dimension of justice but also of human dignity. An equitable and sustainable development is needed.
- *Human rights:* This topic was broadened as well by dealing with the dimensions of liberation, human dignity, the freedom of religions and convictions including the practical dimension of protecting places of worship, the role of children, women, young people and indigenous

---

[93] The Ring for Peace was created and introduced to the Lindau World Assembly by the Foundation Peace Dialogue of the World Religions and Civil Society which was founded in 2018 in Lindau, Germany, by Wolfgang and Monika Schürer, resident in St. Gallen. »The new foundation's aim is to foster the peaceful coexistence between people and religions within Germany and Europe, to strengthen international understanding and cooperation and to promote the dialogue between the generations and nations.« (www.ringforpeace.org).

[94] Vienna, p. 4.

groups. Therefore, the networks of women and youth developed toward a steady element of the organisational structure of Religions for Peace International.

- *Environment:* The issue of protecting the earth came up and was enforced by rising awareness of environmental destruction. Emphasis was among others put on a responsible lifestyle and protection of the rainforest. Respect to nature was underlined as a basic religious attitude.
- Education and awareness building have never been a main headline of an assembly but always an ongoing task.[95]
- Cross cutting topics such as trust, healing, common humanity, well being and shared values played a considerable role and deepened the spiritual and mental dimension of the discourse.

Without a doubt, some of the topics and their reinforcement and further development are reactions to contemporary challenges. This can be seen, for example, from the topic formulation »Welcoming the other«, which responds to growing xenophobia at that time.

By actively dealing with current challenges and by implementing the principals and the visions of a fairer and more peaceful world, Religions for Peace goes partly beyond what is addressed in individual religious communities. Including issues like homosexuality, transgender (LGBT) and sexual education in the new strategic program is surely a step that goes beyond the current consensus in some religious communities. In this sense, Religions for Peace is undoubtedly at the forefront of bringing important issues into the global discourse of religions.

3.5 Ownership and leadership

Religions for Peace International is guided by a »World Council« of around 60 outstanding personalities elected at World Assemblies. »It is comprised of distinguished religious leaders who are dedicated to building peace.«[96]

---

[95] To cope with the issues of education and awareness building Religions for Peace International established a Peace Education Standing Commission (PESC) chaired by Johannes Lähnemann, Germany. For the European context see for example: Lähnemann, Johannes / Schreiner, Peter (ed.), Interreligious and Values Education in Europe: Map and Handbook, Münster/Westf. 2008.

[96] See www.rfp.org.

An Executive Committee, the core group of the World Council, appoints Honorary Presidents to provide leadership in different areas of the movement. International Trustees assist in developing partnerships, providing needed expertise and mobilising resources. The Secretary General, Prof. Dr. Azza Karam[97], is in charge of the office in New York located close to the headquarters of the United Nations. She was elected Secretary General at the 10th World Assembly in Lindau following Dr. William Vendley who assumed leadership of Religions for Peace International in 1994. Prof. Karam is the first woman in this position.

The term »religions« needs to be explained in order to understand the mandate of Religions for Peace and on whose behalf this body can speak. The declaration of the first World Assembly in 1970 states: »We speak for ourselves as persons brought from many religions by our deep concern for peace, we try also to speak for the vast majority of the human family who are powerless and whose voice is seldom heard.«[98] This means that Religions for Peace is not a mandated representation of religious communities but an alliance of representatives from different religions. It should be taken into consideration that numerous religions don't have any organisational form or outstanding representatives who have the mandate or authority to speak in the name of their religion or of their followers. Religions for Peace is very keen to win outstanding religious leaders to serve in boards and committees to profit from their reputation and influence. On the other hand, Religions for Peace consists of a great number of groups on the local and regional level. Members of those groups on the grass-root level are people interested in interreligious dialogue and in supporting the work and objectives of Religions for Peace. Therefore, this organisation can also claim to represent a grass-root movement.

Therefore, the mandate is not derived from a structural representation, but from a shared moral responsibility of those personalities who share the objectives of Religions for Peace and who support this work. »*We as ... a religions people we have a special responsibility for building a peaceful world community.*«[99] This objective, based on a common conviction, also builds

---

[97] Born in Egypt, Azza Karam holds the position of a Professor of Religion and Development in Amsterdam, the Netherlands, where she is a citizen. She has served in different positions in the United Nations since 2004, among others at the United Nations Population Fund (UNFPA), and lives in the United States.

[98] Kyoto 1970, p. 1.

[99] Princeton, p. 1.

a bridge to people outside of religions. Therefore, positions and actions are stated »together with all people of good will«[100]. Religions for Peace is therefore not an organisation with a defined and formal membership, but rather an open alliance or coalition that wants to reach as many people as possible who share the goals.

Against the background of this self-understanding, the declarations and statements of Religions for Peace can also be directed to the religious communities. Phrases like: »We encourage every religion...«; »We call upon all religions...«, »We appeal to religious people...«[101] can be found quite often through the documents.

3.6 Strategic partners

Religions for Peace International – as a non-governmental organisation registered at the United Nations – has sought close contact with the United Nations since it was founded and has set topics and activities in line with the United Nations' agenda. Religions for Peace also saw itself as a »UN of religions«.[102] The first World Assembly stated: »We desire to convey our concern for peace to the United Nations... We urge universal membership in the United Nations.«[103] The United Nations received explicit approval in the Melbourne Declaration[104]. In some cases it is obvious that the choice of the topics was made in reference to the agenda of the United Nations. This might be the case for example when Religions for Peace dealt with the disarmament negotiations particularly in the 1970s and 1980s or with the issue of the state of children.[105]

Numerous international conventions are mentioned, referred to or even initiated by Religions for Peace itself or its partners. This includes the Universal Declaration of Human Rights[106], the Covenant for the Elimination of Intolerance and Discrimination Based on Religion and Belief[107], the United Nations declaration against racism and racial discrimination[108],

---

[100] Riva del Garda, p. 7.
[101] Leuven, p. 2 and 3.
[102] See Dehn, p. 141.
[103] Kyoto 1970, p. 2.
[104] Melbourne, p. 2.
[105] The year of the child was proclaimed by the United Nations in 1976 for the year 1979.
[106] Leuven, p. 3; Princeton, p. 3; Nairobi, p. 3; Melbourne, p. 3.
[107] Princeton, p. 3; Nairobi, p. 4.

the United Nation International Year of the Child[109], the Convention on the rights of the Child[110], the United Nations Declaration of Indigenous Rights[111] and others. Documents which were developed by partners of the Religions for Peace or in conjunction with its network include for example the Peace Charter for Forgiveness and Reconciliation, the Alliance of Virtues, the Faiths for Forest Declaration, the Interfaith Rainforest Initiative and the Universal Code of Conduct on Holy Sites[112].

The Millennium Developments Goals are mentioned in the Kyoto declaration 2006 and the Sustainable Development Goals are – as shown above – an important point of reference in the Strategic Plan 2020–2025. A close connection with the United Nations agenda can also be expected for the years to come as the Secretary General, Prof. Assa Karam, has a strong background from her various activities at the United Nations.

In comparison with the close reference to the Unites Nations, the link to the agendas of the different religious organisations and communities from which the personalities of Religions for Peace are recruited is very small. Conceptual elaborations and activities of the individual religious communities are seldom or not used at all. The reference to a Vietnamese Buddhist campaign in the Leuven Declaration[113] is absolutely singular. Also the reference to Vatican documents in the Workbook to the Lindau Assembly are rare exceptions.

This is all more unfortunate because there are a lot of discourses and activities in the religious communities which could be of great usefulness and support for the topics, statements and the action points of Religions for Peace. To give some examples, the global campaigns of the World Council of Churches (WCC), a fellowship of 350 member churches representing all together more than half a billion Christians around the world, are nowhere mentioned or referred to. The Decade to Overcome Violence was a global program of the World Council of Churches and its member churches in the period from 2001 to 2010. Another example is the global learning process (»Conciliar Process«) of this network on Peace, Justice and the Integrity of Creation which started 1983 in Vancouver and was

---

[108] Princeton, p. 4.
[109] Ibid., p. 4.
[110] Melbourne, p. 2; Riva del Garda, p. 6.
[111] Melbourne, p. 3.
[112] All documents are mentioned in the Lindau Declaration.
[113] Leuven, p. 2.

concluded by a global Ecumenical conference 2010 in Seoul. Both examples cover the topics of Religions for Peace widely. Even the work of aid agencies of the religions as well as practical projects by religious communities are nowhere reflected or referred to in neither the declarations of the World Assemblies nor the current Strategic Plan.

As a result, the Religions for Peace program seems to hover more or less over discourses and efforts in the religions themselves. At least, such contributions from the religious communities are not recognisable. The impression comes up that the Religions for Peace International program leads a certain life of its own, despite the mentioned participatory approach and the work of different commissions. It would be desirable for Religions for Peace to seek a closer, more intensive, or at least a more visible, dialogue including discourses in the religious communities in the future. Both sides could benefit for each other and profit from mutual support.

3.7 Action points and measuring outcomes

The Strategic Plan 2020–2025 explains in its last section[114] an intended monitoring process to measure the outcomes of the 34 action points which are listed in this document. It is promised that this process will be clearly defined in the context of annual plans.[115] It can be assumed that financial support for measures includes the proof of effective use of funds and therefore also the proof of effectiveness or an evaluation of the measures taken. As it is not indicated who will be in charge of the individual projects or whether the respective activities relate to specific locations, countries or continents, the Strategic Plan appears more like a wish list that leaves open which actors will be assigned to individual action points.

In the mentioned section, each activity is assigned to an indicator. In most of the cases the »indicator« means that the number of the respective campaigns or the number of people involved should be recorded. The respective »outcome« is usually defined in such a way that an intensification of the respective activities is expected. This sought outcome is often described in a very vague manner. Action point 1.9 can be an example stating: »*Refugees and migrants are integrated into host society.*« Rather rarely details

---

[114] Strategic Plan, p. 18–23.
[115] Ibid., p. 18.

are specified as in item 2.2 regarding the advancement of women in management positions: *» Women make up 40 percent of RfP leadership.«*

Many of the desired implementations include learning processes, attitudes and soft skills, where it is particularly difficult to measure and quantify success. For such processes, it is recommended to seek cooperation with organisations and research institutions that have developed concepts of »global learning«[116]. The methods of evaluation developed in this context could be very helpful[117] and can also create opportunities for mutual exchange.

Unfortunately, the Strategic Plan does not indicate whether previous action points have been evaluated and what sort of conclusions have been drawn to be taken into consideration for further implementations. Regrettably, there are also no indications in which fields of activities the individual religious communities have already gained experience and how the implementation of strategic goals could be made more effective through coordination or division of labour among them.

4. The benefit of inter-religious cooperation

There is no doubt that the collaboration of representatives of different religious traditions marks an important step forward in promoting peaceful coexistence and reducing tensions, hostility and conflicts. In a broader historical context, such cooperation, in particular on a global level, can be described as an important civilizational step forward of mankind. In addition, this applies also to the common goal to work for peace in a very broad understanding. The discourse to identify basic convictions of »common humanity« are not only convictions based on deeper insight, reason and conscience, but they are also »widely shared values« in the sense that they encompass the global challenges in their geographical dimension.

The discourse that has been described here based on the history of Religions for Peace from its foundation up to today is very closely interwoven

---

[116] See for example: Bourn, Douglas (ed), The Bloomsbury Handbook of Global Education and Learning, London / New York / Oxford / New Delhi / Sydney 2020.

[117] See Scheunpflug, Annette, Evidence and Efficacy. A Compulsion for Global Education?, in: Bourn 2020, p. 40–51.

with the discourse in numerous other movements and organisations, especially with the developments in the area of the United Nations. Against this background the question should be raised in this last section what particular contribution religions can make to this discourse and what the surplus, the benefit and the advantage of multi-religious cooperation are. I would like to answer these questions in four theses.

4.1 More effective through multi-religious cooperation

The first answer is the general insight that working together can increase impact and effects. This is expressed in the declaration of the Kyoto World Assembly in 2006 as follows:

»The efforts of individual religious communities are made vastly more effective through multi-religious cooperation. Religious communities working together can be powerful actors to prevent violence before it erupts.«[118]

Cooperation is an advantage not only by being numerically stronger to reinforce impacts or to achieve goals, but also by creating a sense of community and agreement when acting in common. This includes avoiding conflicts and tensions that hinder the achievement of the envisaged goals. The cooperation between religious communities as such on an international level also creates a platform and offers the opportunity to address and deal with conflicts that exist at the local or regional level. This is of particular importance for endangered and vulnerable religious and other minorities. Religion for Peace International tries to play this role when mediations and peace talks are offered for conflict settlement. This higher level of mediation offers the possibility of a neutral and non-partisan position. But religious mediators have often little political power and are dependent on the willingness to communicate of those involved.

4.2 Religious contribution to the development of global values

The profile of Religions for Peace, focusing on the vision of a comprehensive peace, is more or less based on three sources.

---

[118] Kyoto 2006, p. 3.

On the one hand, there are fundamental values, teachings and beliefs of religious communities, from their scriptures and traditions. Bringing this to bear into societies is often referred to as a »moral mandate«. The second is the insight from reason and conscience, which in the current historical situation can only be thought and developed in a global horizon. The reference to human rights marks a global discourse on fundamental convictions and values. The third are challenges which can constantly come up in new historical situations and that can change in their weight. In the 1980s, the nuclear threat was an all-encompassing danger of »human overkill«. The ecological disaster, including climate change, has become an almost more comprehensive threat scenario. The Corona pandemic, which broke out at the end of 2019 and spread rapidly worldwide, highlights a new dimension of global threat and illustrates once again how much the fate of people in one country is linked to and depending on the fate of everyone.

In the interplay of these three factors, answers from the teachings of the religious communities are sought, using reason and conscience to global challenges. This is a search process that also results in an ever-changing terminology in the Religions for Peace documents[119]. It was stated above that this process can be understood as something like an ethical »à qui«, i.e. the current status of a comprehensive discourse, which is open to the future, since new challenges always have to be reconsidered.

By participating in this discourse and implementing the beliefs and strategic insights that have been achieved, the representatives from the religious communities working together in Religions for Peace want to assume moral responsibility at the global level. By performing this responsibility in relation to governmental and supranational organisations, they become indeed »global civil actors«.

---

[119] Confer the above mentioned terms like »moral mandate«, »modern order« or »widely shared values«.

4.3 Learning processes for religious communities

The global discourse involves the religious communities in a learning process.[120] The personalities and groups from different religious traditions working together in Religions for Peace play a pioneering role. However, it is also evident that large parts of the religious communities are in no way facing the current global challenges and are hesitant to examine their beliefs accordingly.

The role of women can serve as an example. Religions for Peace has long been committed to strengthening the role of women, seeks to extend their presence in management positions and is taking action to combat violence against women. Although such positions and actions are similarly shared and carried out by individual religious communities, it should be noted at the same time that there are certain religious traditions and doctrines that continue to hold on to male dominance and to keep women away from, for example, priestly functions from achieving equality in public life or from reviewing the inheritance law.

The »widely shared values« represented by Religions for Peace must initiate a discourse and a process of self-examination especially in the religious communities themselves. If bigger parts of the religious communities do not agree to the widely shared values in their teachings, their religious traditions and in the everyday life of their members, it will be difficult to represent such positions credibly as the basis for common convictions and activities of multi-religious cooperation.

4.4 The dialectic of communality and plurality

Religions for Peace does not consider itself as a lobby group in the sense of interests and rights of religious communities being represented and sued. Striving for freedom of thought, conscience and religion as one of the areas of concern of Religions for Peace in general and of its Strategic Plan 2020–2025[121] in particular, cannot be considered as an effort in lobby-

---

[120] Concerning the significance of globalisation for religious education see for example Simojoki, Henrik, Globalisierte Religion. Ausgangspunkte, Maßstäbe und Perspektiven religiöser Bildung in der Weltgesellschaft (Globalized religion. Starting points, standards and perspectives of religious education in world society), Tübingen 2012.

[121] Strategic Plan, p. 15f; field S4 of the »goal implementation«.

ing or for reasons of self-interest. Rather, it is part of the general promotion of human rights. Concerning this item, the Strategic Plan refers to Article 18 of the Universal Declaration of Human Rights and the aim »to advance a more robust notion of citizenship«.[122]

This shows two dialectic settings. First, the »shared values« are rooted in religious traditions and basic components of their teaching and their ethical convictions, but these »shared values« are also a critical counterpart vis-à-vis the convictions and tendencies in the area of religions which are in contradiction to these principals. Second, the value of tolerance and the freedom of thought, conscience and religion are convictions which require universal approval but acknowledge at the same time the plurality of convictions, beliefs and thoughts. This implies that the balance of unity and plurality, of common convictions and different traditions and beliefs must always be observed and found anew.

The example of the Grand Mughal Akbar mentioned in the introduction of this article shows clearly that the noble intention of uniting different traditions and groupings under one basic belief will fail if the balance between common principles and freedom of beliefs and convictions is not kept.

This means that today a »multi-lingual« qualification is needed: the language of global responsibility and the commitment to a »shared well-being« – in taking up the title of the Lindau World Assembly – and the languages of a vast richness of numerous religious traditions and beliefs as a resource for discovering and reinterpreting their wisdom to respond to today's and tomorrow's challenges.

---

[122] Ibid., p. 15.

The Author

Rev. Dr. theol. Martin Affolderbach, born 1947; studied Protestant theology in Wuppertal, Heidelberg and Bonn; doctorate at the University of Bonn; reverend of the Protestant Church in the Rhineland; parish pastor in Bielefeld (1976–1978); policy and study officer of the Federation of Protestant Youth (aej), Stuttgart (1979–1986); director of the conference and training center for Protestant youthwork (Jugendakademie), Radevormwald (1987–1995); secretary for migration and asylum issues and inter-religious affairs in the national church office of the Protestant Church in Germany (EKD), Hanover (1995–2012); retired in 2013 and moved to Nuremberg; different teaching assignments at colleges and universities in Bielefeld, Bochum, Erlangen, Nürnberg, Bamberg and Butare/Rwanda.

His teaching assignments as lecturer at the University of Bamberg include concepts and practices of inter-religious co-operation, recently carried out in cooperation with international partners from the Religions for Peace network. This contributes to the remarkable tradition of this topic at the University of Bamberg.

For further information on activities, teaching and publications see www.affolderbach.de